KATIE QUINN DAVIES began her career as a graphic
designer, then, in 2009 focused her creative energies on
food photography and soon her blog, 'What Katie Ate',
was born. It became an internet phenomenon with
a huge following in Australia, Europe and the U.S.
When she's not shooting advertising and editorial features
for leading food and lifestyle magazines and advertising
clients from her Sydney studio, Katie loves to cook and
update the blog with a variety of new and seasonal recipes.

whatkatieate.com

WHAT KATIE ATE

at the weekend...

Photography by
Katie Quinn Davies

SALT · YARD
BOOK C°

This book is affectionately dedicated to all my
stupendously amazing friends and family and,
in particular, Alix, Lou and Madeleine · there's no way
I could have done this without you, I love you all
loads. You're all supercalifragilisticexpialidocious :) x

INTRODUCTION

The past two years, since the release of my first book *What Katie Ate*, have been a massive whirlwind for me. I pinch myself sometimes when I realise the book has sold into almost twenty countries worldwide and been translated into ten languages. I love it when yet another foreign edition turns up in the mail and I see my recipes translated into Italian, Portuguese, French, Russian or German. So I was thrilled to be asked to write a follow-up, and to continue on this relatively new journey as a cookbook writer, photographer, stylist, designer (and all the other gazillion hats I wear to make this dream a reality, somewhat single-handedly!).

This book is all about weekend eating and what I love best — cooking food for my family and friends. I've always said one of my favourite things to do is throw a great dinner party or a barbecue during the warmer months here in Sydney, and that hasn't changed. I get enormous enjoyment from cooking for the masses, and I love the whole process, from the planning to the serving, before watching my mates dig in. To me, one of the best things in life is to enjoy good food and good wine with those closest to you. Breaking bread with friends, so to speak.

I'm super-happy with these recipes, which have been inspired by so many wonderful experiences, from my own experimentation in the kitchen, to meals enjoyed on my travels over the past two years and recipes borrowed from friends. The dishes include ideas for lazy brunch get-togethers, lavish dinner parties, cocktail party food and drinks, textural salads and beautiful marinated or slow-cooked meats. They're not just good for weekends, either — many can easily be whipped up for a midweek meal.

I've learnt so much about food and writing recipes over the past couple of years, mainly due to my time spent doing a monthly column for *delicious.* magazine. Every month I would write, test, cook, style and shoot a collection of recipes for the magazine based on a seasonal theme. It taught me a lot about seasonal produce and putting flavours together, and I had great fun doing it. I've included a few of those dishes here, as well as a handful of favourites from my blog, *whatkatieate.com*.

Since the first book was published, I've done quite a bit of travelling: to Tokyo (amazing!), the US, Italy, London, Ireland and around Australia. Finding inspiration in meals I've eaten with friends and family on my travels is probably my favourite way to come up with recipe ideas — I love trying to work out what might be in each dish and experimenting in the kitchen when I get home, often combining one or two recipes and putting my own spin on them. The sliders on pages 236–239 are a perfect example of this.

For this book, I have included loads of photos of weekends enjoyed in my hometown of Dublin (see pages 76–85), the beautiful Barossa Valley with its wonderfully warm people (see pages 32–41), and *Italia* – my favourite country in the world (see pages 142–151). Plus, there's also some weekends spent back home in Sydney: a girly get-together with some of my Aussie blog readers (see pages 178–185 – thanks again, girls!), and a party at my house with a bit of Mexican flair (see pages 250–257).

The highlight of these past few years was, without a doubt, travelling to New York and winning the coveted James Beard Award for Best Photography and being nominated for Best General Cookbook in May 2013. I don't think I've ever been as shocked in my life as when I woke up one morning to a plethora of tweets congratulating me on my nominations; I was totally stunned, yet utterly thrilled and crazy excited. The awards are the Oscars of the culinary world in the US and I was honoured (and just a bit gobsmacked) to have been chosen as a finalist alongside many high-calibre people from the world of American cookery, media and publishing.

For a while, I tossed up whether or not to go to the ceremony, but I knew in my heart of hearts it was a no-brainer, so plane tickets and hotel were duly booked and – in typical girly fashion – deliberations regarding dress/shoes/bag/accessories/hair and make-up began! The evening arrived and there I was, sitting at the awards table in Gotham Hall with my US publisher Megan. When my name was called out as a nomination for Best Photography I was a bag of nerves, and even more so when I heard my name called out again as the winner: I nearly died with excitement! I have great recollections of walking what felt like about two miles through the grand dining room to the stage, being high-fived by a load of strangers en route. After a nervously mumbled acceptance speech – something about the luck of the Irish – I was whisked away to have my photo taken, complete with a glass of champers which I almost slopped onto the floor because my hands were shaking so badly. It was an incredible experience and I will always be grateful to the judges who voted for my book and to the James Beard Foundation.

My goal with this book was to produce a cookbook that would be familiar to my readers, but with a lighter, brighter feel – a reflection of my life here in Sydney and the food I love to eat and serve. I guess this book is a journal of my recipe writing and travels over the past two years, with a few behind-the-scenes shots included to show the real 'glamour' of a frantic food shoot!

I have really enjoyed writing and shooting this book, although it's been a much bigger undertaking than my first. Sure, it was tough and super-stressful at times, but I am incredibly proud of the end result. I hope that you find lots of recipes to enjoy with your own family and friends, and continue to follow my work.

With love
Katie x

BREAKFA

AND

BRUNCH

SPECIAL BLACK PEPPER
"GRAN DI CAPRA"
(GOAT CHEESE)

ZUBAIq
(GOAT)
£ 50,00 /Kg

OAT CHEESE
onths matured
30,00 per Kg

CROTONE
YEARS OLD

BEST
ORINO
THE

ICATA (GOAT)
0,00 per Kg

FRESH PECORINO
£28.00 Kg

ORGANIC GOAT CHEESE
£ 25,00 per Kg

GO
8

SPECIAL GOAT CHEESE
4 months matured
conserved in STRAW
£ 30.00 per Kg

KATIE'S GRANOLA WITH BLUEBERRY COMPOTE AND YOGHURT

Serves 4–6

Homemade granola is one of the easiest things to make; I love to whip up a batch on a Sunday evening and use it throughout the week. The nut, seed and berry mix will keep in an airtight container for up to 2 weeks. Puffed quinoa and chia seeds are available from health food stores, and light agave nectar (a plant-derived sweetener) can be found at health food stores and gourmet delis.

140 g hazelnuts
80 g almonds
75 g sunflower seeds
50 g pumpkin seeds
2 tablespoons light agave nectar
50 g dried cranberries
50 g dried blueberries
30 g goji berries
25 g puffed quinoa
2 tablespoons chia seeds
560 g natural yoghurt

BLUEBERRY COMPOTE
250 g blueberries
2 tablespoons light agave nectar
2 teaspoons lime juice

Preheat the oven to 200°C/180°C fan/gas 6 and line a baking tray with greaseproof paper.

Combine the nuts and seeds in a bowl, then pour over the agave nectar and stir to coat. Spread out evenly on the prepared tray and bake for 8–10 minutes or until golden brown and toasted. Remove and set aside to cool completely, then transfer to a large bowl, breaking up any larger pieces. Add the dried berries, quinoa and chia seeds and stir to combine. (Makes about 500 g.)

For the blueberry compote, place all the ingredients and 1 tablespoon water in a small saucepan and bring to a boil over high heat. Reduce the heat to low and simmer, stirring often, for 2–3 minutes or until the berries are soft. Drain the fruit, reserving the liquid, and set aside. Simmer the reserved liquid over low heat for 4–5 minutes or until reduced by half. Pour this over the berries and leave to cool.

To serve, divide the compote among bowls or jars, add a layer of yoghurt and finish with the nut, seed and berry mix.

THE
MOST FLAVORFUL
AND CREAMIEST

SUPER SMOOTHIES

Serves 2 {Makes 700 ml}

Honestly, I've never been much of a fan of the
super-healthy 'green shakes' that are so popular
nowadays, but this one tastes fantastic. It contains kale,
which ordinarily would make some people run for
the hills screaming, but it's virtually undetectable in
the finished drink. This is a great one to make for the
kids, to get their leafy greens into them on the sly . . .

2 kiwifruit, peeled
1 green apple, cored
20 g kale or baby spinach leaves
2 teaspoons lemon juice
1 small handful mint
1 large handful ice, plus extra to serve

Put all the ingredients and 250 ml cold water into
a blender and whiz until smooth.

Pour into chilled glasses, add extra ice and serve.

SARDINES ON TOAST WITH TARRAGON AND LEMON MAYO

Serves 4

These are great for a weekend brunch with friends. I like to remove the bones from sardines, but you can leave them in if you like — they are tiny, and full of calcium!

250 g cherry tomatoes
sea salt and freshly ground black pepper
16 fresh sardines, cleaned and scaled (ask your fishmonger to do this for you)
1 tablespoon plain flour, sifted
1 tablespoon rice flour, sifted
finely grated zest of 2 lemons
olive oil or rice bran oil, for shallow-frying
4 free-range eggs
buttered wholegrain sourdough toast and dill sprigs, to serve

TARRAGON AND LEMON MAYO
3 free-range egg yolks
2 tablespoons lemon juice
sea salt
125 ml rapeseed oil
2 teaspoons tarragon vinegar
1 teaspoon Dijon mustard
2 teaspoons salted capers, well rinsed
1 small handful dill
freshly ground white pepper

Preheat the oven to 200°C/180°C fan/gas 6 and line a baking tray with greaseproof paper.

Place the tomatoes on the prepared tray, season with a little salt and roast for 20 minutes or until the skins start to burst.

Meanwhile, for the mayo, place the egg yolks, lemon juice and a pinch of salt in the bowl of a food processor. Process on high speed for 1 minute then, with the motor running, add the oil in a thin, steady stream until the mixture is thick and glossy. Add the vinegar, mustard, capers, dill and white pepper and process again until just combined, then cover and set aside.

Pat the sardines dry with kitchen roll.

Place the sifted flours, lemon zest, a pinch of salt and a good seasoning of black pepper in a shallow bowl and stir to combine. Add the sardines and toss to coat well.

Fill a large, deep saucepan with oil to a depth of 5 mm and heat over medium–high heat. Shallow-fry the sardines for a minute or two on each side until cooked through and golden brown. Remove with a slotted spoon and drain on kitchen roll. Set aside and keep warm.

Fill a saucepan with water and heat to 80°C or until just barely simmering. Working with one egg at a time, crack the eggs onto a slotted spoon (allowing any watery egg white to run off), then slide the egg into the simmering water. Cook for 4 minutes, then remove with the slotted spoon and drain on kitchen roll. Cover and keep warm while you cook the remaining eggs.

Place a piece of toast on each plate and top with the tomatoes, sardines, egg and some mayo. Finish with a good grinding of pepper and garnish with dill.

CHOCOLATE AND SOUR CHERRY HOTCAKES

These hotcakes are great for a special weekend breakfast or brunch. You could also serve them as a dessert if you like. I use frozen sour cherries in the batter, but you can opt for the morello ones that come in a jar (just drain them well before use) or, even better, use fresh if they're in season. Toast the slivered almonds in the oven for 6–8 minutes at 200°C/180°C/gas 6, keeping an eye on them to make sure they don't burn. Buckwheat flour is available from health food stores.

300 g buckwheat flour
2 teaspoons baking powder
2 teaspoons bicarbonate of soda
½ teaspoon ground cinnamon
1 tablespoon cocoa powder (optional)
500 ml buttermilk
1 large free-range egg
60 g butter, melted, plus extra for cooking
2 tablespoons light agave nectar (see page 10), plus extra to serve (optional)
300 g frozen sour cherries, thawed and drained on kitchen roll
200 g creme fraiche
200 g fresh cherries, halved and pitted (or use drained bottled cherries)
50 g slivered almonds, toasted and chopped

Makes 16

Preheat the oven to 150°C/130°C fan/gas 2 and line a baking tray with greaseproof paper.

Sift the dry ingredients into a large bowl and set aside.

Whisk the buttermilk, egg, melted butter and agave nectar together in a jug.

Make a well in the centre of the dry ingredients and pour in the wet ingredients. Using a wooden spoon, beat everything together until combined, then fold in the thawed cherries.

Melt ½ teaspoon butter in a large non-stick crepe or frying pan over medium heat. Add three portions of batter to the pan (about 3 tablespoons each), and cook for 2–3 minutes or until browned underneath. Carefully flip the hotcakes and cook for 2–3 minutes on the other side, then transfer to the prepared tray and keep them warm in the oven while you continue with the remaining batter, adding ½ teaspoon butter to the pan to cook each batch.

Sandwich the hotcakes together with creme fraiche. Top each stack with a final dollop of creme fraiche, the halved cherries, almonds and an extra drizzle of agave nectar, if using.

MUSHROOM, SPINACH AND CHEESE OMELETTE

This is my 'fluffy' omelette, made by whizzing the eggs in a blender to give a light and airy texture to the final dish. Serve this with buttered toast, if you like.

3 free-range eggs
3 tablespoons milk
sea salt
25 g butter, plus extra for cooking
50 g shiitake mushrooms, sliced or left whole if small
50 g chestnut mushrooms, sliced
2 sprigs thyme, leaves stripped
freshly ground black pepper
15 g baby spinach leaves
30 g emmental cheese, finely sliced

Serves 1–2

Place the eggs, milk and a pinch of salt in a blender and whiz for 30–40 seconds or until combined and fluffy, then set aside.

Melt the butter in a non-stick frying pan over high heat. Add the mushrooms and most of the thyme, saving a little for the garnish, then season well and cook for 4–5 minutes or until the mushrooms are just tender. Transfer to a plate and keep warm.

Wipe the pan clean and melt a little extra butter over low heat. Pour in the egg mixture and cook for 4–5 minutes or until it starts to set around the edges. Add the mushrooms, spinach and cheese to one half, then fold the remaining half over the filling and cook for 1–2 minutes. Flip the omelette over and cook for 1 minute or until just cooked. Turn out onto a plate, sprinkle over the remaining thyme and serve immediately.

MANDARIN, PISTACHIO AND POPPY-SEED MUFFINS

№. 20

These are brilliant for breakfast-on-the-run or a snack at work – make a batch on a Sunday night and you're sorted for a few days. Just remember to check your teeth for poppy seeds before you smile at your boss!

4 mandarins
300 g plain flour
2 teaspoons baking powder
2 teaspoons ground cinnamon
120 g brown sugar
fine salt
4 large free-range eggs
120 g unsalted butter, melted and cooled slightly
2 teaspoons orange flower water
140 g pistachios, shelled and coarsely chopped
1 tablespoon poppy seeds

Makes 10 large muffins

Preheat the oven to 200°C/180°C fan/gas 6. Cut out ten squares of greaseproof paper and use to line ten 250 ml holes of a muffin tin.

Finely grate the zest of one mandarin and set aside. Peel and segment the mandarins, removing any excess pith and seeds (you'll need 350 g mandarin segments). Cut the segments in half and set aside.

Sift the flour, baking powder, cinnamon, sugar and a pinch of salt into a large bowl and stir to combine.

Lightly whisk the eggs together in another bowl. Stir in the cooled melted butter, orange flower water and reserved mandarin zest, then pour this mixture into the dry ingredients and combine with a wooden spoon.

Set aside a handful of mandarin pieces for the garnish and add the rest to the batter, along with two-thirds of the pistachios and three-quarters of the poppy seeds. Gently fold everything together.

Spoon the batter into the lined muffin holes and top each with some reserved mandarin pieces. Scatter the remaining pistachios and poppy seeds over the top.

Bake for 25–30 minutes or until a skewer inserted in the centres comes out almost dry. Leave the muffins to cool slightly in the tin before lifting out onto a wire rack and cooling completely.

CHORIZO ROSTI WITH DUCK EGGS AND ANCHOVY MAYO

This is inspired by a meal I enjoyed on a recent trip to New York that featured ramps, a popular North American vegetable with an oniony, garlicky flavour. If you can't get duck eggs, use four large free-range eggs instead. Serve this with roasted tomatoes, if you like.

800 g potatoes, scrubbed and coarsely grated
25 g butter, melted
sea salt and freshly ground black pepper
olive oil or rice bran oil, for cooking
1 brown onion, finely chopped
4 cloves garlic, 2 finely chopped, 2 cut in half
220 g good-quality chorizo sausages, finely diced
2 bunches spring onions, white and pale green parts only, halved lengthways
4 free-range duck eggs
snipped dill, to garnish

ANCHOVY MAYO
2 free-range egg yolks
1 tablespoon lemon juice
sea salt
125 ml rapeseed oil
2 teaspoons Dijon mustard
1 tablespoon white wine vinegar
2 large anchovies, chopped
1 teaspoon Worcestershire sauce
freshly ground white pepper

Place the grated potato in a clean tea towel, then wrap up and squeeze hard to wring out as much excess water as possible. Place the potato in a large bowl with the melted butter, salt and pepper and toss to coat thoroughly, then set aside.

Heat 1 tablespoon oil in a large non-stick frying pan over medium–high heat, then add the onion and chopped garlic and cook for 4–5 minutes until softened. Transfer to the bowl with the potato mixture.

Heat 2 teaspoons oil in the same pan over medium heat, then add the chorizo and cook for 3–4 minutes, stirring, until just browned. Add this to the potato mixture and toss to combine well.

Preheat the oven to 200°C/180°C fan/gas 6 and line a baking tray with greaseproof paper.

Wipe the pan clean with kitchen roll, then add 1 tablespoon oil and place over medium–high heat. Spoon one-quarter of the potato mixture in the pan and shape roughly into a circle. Flatten with a spatula and cook for 1–2 minutes until browned, then flip over and cook for a further 2 minutes. Transfer to the prepared tray and repeat with the remaining mixture to make four rostis in total, adding more oil to the pan as needed.

Place the tray in the oven and bake the rostis for 20–25 minutes or until golden brown, crisp and cooked through.

Meanwhile, for the mayo, place the egg yolks, lemon juice and a pinch of salt in a food processor. Process on high speed for 1 minute, then, with the motor running, add the oil in a thin, steady stream until thick and glossy. Add the remaining ingredients and process for 30 seconds to combine, then cover and set aside until needed.

Heat 1 tablespoon oil in the frying pan over medium heat, add the halved garlic cloves and cook for 1 minute, stirring often, then remove the garlic and discard. Add the spring onion to the pan and cook, tossing, for 3–4 minutes or until light golden-brown and slightly softened. Remove from the pan and cover to keep warm.

Wipe the pan clean again and heat 1 tablespoon oil over medium–high heat. Working in batches depending on the size of your pan, crack the eggs into the pan and cook for 2 minutes, then cover with a lid and cook for 1½ minutes until the underside is crisp and the yolk is still runny.

Top each rosti with spring onion and an egg, then drizzle with mayonnaise, season and scatter with dill to finish.

Serves 4

BAKED EGGS IN PUFF PASTRY CUPS

These are impressively flavoursome given the few ingredients involved. Try to use the best pastry you can: I use Carême, which is an Australian-made pastry that gives excellent results. The truffle oil is optional in this dish, but it's a wonderful addition.

2 sheets puff pastry (25 cm × 25 cm), thawed if frozen
2 tablespoons milk
1 free-range egg yolk
8 thin slices prosciutto, halved lengthways
8 free-range eggs
90 g grated gruyere, plus extra to serve
white truffle oil (optional), snipped chives and freshly
    ground black pepper, to serve

Makes 8

Preheat the oven to 200°C/180°C fan/gas 6 and grease eight holes of a muffin tin.

Cut the pastry into eight 12.5 cm squares and use to line the muffin holes, pleating and folding the pastry as necessary to form a cup. Press any overlapping pastry to an even thickness. Prick all over with a fork.

Cut out eight squares of greaseproof paper slightly larger than the pastry squares. Scrunch up the paper, then smooth it out and use to line the pastry bases. Fill with baking beans or rice and blind-bake for 10 minutes. Remove the paper and beans or rice and bake for a further 10 minutes or until the bases are cooked.

Whisk together the milk and egg yolk, then brush over the bases. Line each base with two thin strips of prosciutto, then crack an egg into each one and sprinkle with cheese.

Bake for 12–15 minutes or until the pastry is golden and the egg is set. Leave to cool slightly in the tin, then remove and serve topped with a drizzle of truffle oil (if using), some snipped chives and a grinding of pepper. Top with extra grated cheese to finish.

APPLE AND ALMOND PASTRIES

These are my take on homemade rough-and-ready French pastries – great with coffee for a Sunday brunch. Use bought wholemeal or gluten-free pastry if you prefer.

150 g honey, plus extra for drizzling
2 tablespoons maple syrup
½ teaspoon ground ginger
1½ teaspoons ground cinnamon
2 teaspoons vanilla-bean paste
150 g almonds, toasted and coarsely chopped
3 green apples, peeled, cored and cut into 1.5 cm dice, then combined with the juice of ½ lemon
1 free-range egg yolk, mixed with a little milk
toasted flaked almonds, to serve

ROUGH PUFF PASTRY
250 g unsalted butter, chilled and cubed
125 g wholemeal plain flour, sifted, plus extra for sprinkling
125 g plain flour, sifted
fine salt

Makes 18

For the pastry, place 200 g of the cubed butter in the freezer to keep really chilled. Place the flours and a good pinch of salt in the bowl of a food processor and pulse to combine. Add the remaining 50 g butter and pulse until incorporated.

Add the butter from the freezer and pulse once or twice, then add 2½ tablespoons cold water and pulse once. Add another 2½ tablespoons cold water and pulse once or twice to just bring together.

Scrape the dough onto a lightly floured surface and sprinkle a little flour on top. Using your hands, squeeze and shape the dough into a cylinder, then wrap in cling film and refrigerate for 30 minutes.

Roll out the chilled dough on a lightly floured surface to a 50 cm ×x 25 cm rectangle.

With the short side facing you, fold the top third of the dough two-thirds of the way down, then fold the bottom third up and over that. Give the dough a quarter-turn and roll out again to the original rectangle shape. Repeat this process four or five times, wrapping the dough in cling

film and refrigerating for 15 minutes after every second turn so it remains easy to handle. When the folding and rolling is complete, wrap the dough in cling film and refrigerate for 2 hours.

Preheat the oven to 200°C/180°C fan/gas 6 and line two baking trays with greaseproof paper.

Roll out the chilled dough on a lightly floured surface to a 50 cm square.

Combine the honey, maple syrup, ginger, cinnamon and vanilla-bean paste in a small bowl. Using a spatula, spread the mixture over the pastry sheet, leaving a 3 cm border. Scatter over the chopped nuts and apple. Carefully roll up like a Swiss roll as tightly as you can without breaking the pastry. Brush all over with egg wash.

Using a very sharp knife, cut the roll into 2 cm slices. Lay the slices on the prepared trays at 2 cm intervals, drizzle with a little extra honey and scatter with toasted flaked almonds. Bake for 25–30 minutes or until golden brown.

Serve warm or cold.

MEXICAN BEEF AND EGGS

Chipotle sauce and fresh jalapenos were once only found in the US, but are now fairly widely available from greengrocers and some supermarkets. I use Goya chipotle sauce: it's not too strong and comes in a decent-sized bottle.

1 tablespoon olive oil
1 onion, finely chopped
sea salt
400 g lean minced free-range beef
60 ml chipotle sauce
1 × 400 g tin chopped tomatoes
1 large handful coriander, coarsely chopped, plus extra to serve
freshly ground black pepper
4 free-range eggs
1 jalapeno chilli, thinly sliced

Serves 4

Heat the oil in a large wide saucepan over medium–high heat. Add the onion and a pinch of salt and cook, stirring often, for 3–4 minutes or until soft. Increase the heat to high, add the beef and cook, stirring occasionally, for 5 minutes or until browned, breaking up any lumps as you go. Stir in the chipotle sauce, tomatoes and coriander, season with salt and pepper, then reduce the heat to medium and cook for 5–6 minutes or until slightly thickened.

Using a spoon, make four indents in the mince mixture and crack an egg into each. Cover and cook for 5–7 minutes or until the eggs and mince are cooked. Garnish with sliced chilli and extra coriander, then grind some black pepper over and serve immediately.

BUCKWHEAT CREPES WITH SPINACH AND RICOTTA

This light meal is healthy and very tasty, with a lovely combination of textures. Hot sauce is available from selected gourmet delis and supermarkets.

300 g buckwheat flour
sea salt and freshly ground black pepper
1 large free-range egg
930 ml milk
light olive oil or rapeseed oil spray
light sour cream, hot sauce and mint leaves, to serve

RICOTTA FILLING
240 g fresh ricotta
225 g baby spinach leaves
4 spring onions, trimmed, white and green parts finely chopped
1 large handful mint, finely chopped
40 g pine nuts, toasted

Serves 6–8

Preheat the oven to 150°C/130°C fan/gas 2 and line a baking tray with greaseproof paper.

Place the flour and a pinch of salt in a large mixing bowl. Add the egg and 60 ml of the milk and whisk together to combine. Pour in the remaining milk, whisking constantly until smooth. Season with pepper and pour into a jug.

Spray a non-stick 20 cm crepe or frying pan with a little oil and heat over high heat. When hot, ladle in just under 60 ml batter and swirl the pan so that the batter coats the base evenly. Cook for 40–50 seconds or until browned around the edges, then flip with a spatula and cook for a further 30 seconds. Transfer to the prepared tray and keep warm in the oven while you cook the remaining batter; you'll get about twenty-four crepes.

Meanwhile, for the filling, place all the ingredients in a bowl and mix together. Season to taste and set aside.

To assemble, spread a thick layer of sour cream on each crepe and top with a tablespoon of filling. Add a splash of hot sauce and garnish with mint leaves, then roll up the crepes and serve.

Menu

POST CARD
CARTE POSTALE

Roast chicken with bacon, kale and almond stuffing page **105**

Roast pork with cider and maple syrup page **118**

Roast vegetables with goat's curd and hazelnuts page **164**

Smashed potatoes with rosemary page **160**

Just before I left to go to Europe in the winter of 2013 (I'm still getting used to the fact that June to August is winter in Australia – those months will always be summer ones to me…), I was booked on a photography job in the Barossa Valley, just north of Adelaide in South Australia. It's predominantly a winemaking region, and it's a place I have totally fallen in love with – not just because of its beauty and stunning natural surroundings, but also the people. They are probably the warmest, friendliest, most hospitable people I have met in this incredible country.

I was there to shoot a selection of local artisan food producers, including cheesemakers, farmers, pickle makers, smoked meats producers, noodle makers, winemakers and restaurateurs. One of these was an amazing woman called Jan Angas. Jan and her husband John farm sheep and run a vineyard called Hutton Vale,

BAROSSA VALLEY

and their cellar door was just mind-blowing. I was left slack-jawed when I drove up to it, and even more so when I explored the many outbuildings and the main house. They were full of everything vintage and there was a powerful sense of history and love about the place. I found it impossible not to snap away for hours, in between shooting Jan and her produce. I just knew I'd have to return here one day to do a shoot for my next book.

So, in October 2013, I went back to the Barossa to stay with Michael Wohlstadt. Michael is one of the most welcoming people you'll ever meet. He runs a free-range pig farm and dairy, as well as a stunning guesthouse called Dairyman's Cottage. I took much delight in furiously photographing all his baby piggies and pottering around his farm, building up a great collection of images. Over at the guesthouse I was greeted with a stunning breakfast tray full of the best local produce, as well as meats, cheeses and wine. We enjoyed a few glasses of red that night, accompanied by his incredible toasted spiced almonds (see recipe page 220).

continued overleaf…

PULLETS

FOR SALE

The next day I was up early to go to the Barossa Farmers' market, where I stocked up on the best of the local produce: free-range organic chickens from Saskia Beer (Maggie's daughter), vegetables, cheeses and breads. I then headed to Hutton Vale to whip up a thank you lunch for all those I had met on my earlier trip. It was outstanding, and I was blown away by everyone being so willing and eager to chip in and help me prepare the feast. I fondly remember standing in the kitchen, watching my guests chopping veggies, making breadcrumbs, preparing the meat and just generally being amazingly supportive and kind. After a few hours of prep and cooking, we all sat down (well, all except me, as I was snapping like crazy for an hour or two!) to enjoy the food and wine. We had a ball and the fun lasted long into the wee hours as bottle after bottle of superb Hutton Vale wine was generously produced by John. I have the most wonderful memories of sitting around the outdoor fire surrounded by so many amazing people who I hope will be friends for life.

Places I stayed and websites of interest:

huttonvale.com
barossaheritagepork.com.au
dairymanscottage.com.au
barossafarmersmarket.com.au
saskiabeer.com

HUTTON VALE

HN LBS
1ST X LBS
LBS FX
CRUTCHINGS
CATARPO
C PA
RFA

McDONALD Imperial
ROTAMATIC RELAY PULSATION
MILKING MACHINE

SALADS AND SOUPS

BULGAR WHEAT AND HERBS WITH SEMI-DRIED TOMATOES

Bulgar wheat is an ingredient I only started using
recently after it was the feature of a photoshoot
I did for US magazine *Eating Well*. It has got a wonderful
texture, and is most commonly found in the classic
Middle-Eastern salad tabbouleh. For a gluten-free
option, use white quinoa instead.

6 plum tomatoes, quartered
sea salt and freshly ground black pepper
olive oil spray
160 g coarse bulgar wheat
70 g pumpkin seeds
40 g flaked almonds
1 large handful mint, finely chopped
1 large handful basil, finely chopped

Serves 4 as a side

Preheat the oven to 150°C/130°C fan/gas 2 and line a
baking tray with greaseproof paper.

Place the tomatoes on the tray, season and spray with
a little oil. Roast for 2 hours, or until semi-dried and
just starting to brown around the edges.

Meanwhile, place the bulgar wheat in a bowl and pour
in 625 ml cold water. Set aside for 1 hour, then drain,
rinse and squeeze out any excess water.
Set aside until needed.

Scatter the pumpkin seeds and flaked almonds on
another baking tray, then place in the oven with the
tomatoes and cook for 12 minutes or until lightly
toasted. Remove and set aside to cool.

Place all the ingredients in a large bowl, season well
and mix to combine, then serve.

SMOKED TROUT, EGG AND POTATO SALAD

The ingredients in this salad work incredibly well together.
Any leftover mayo will keep in an airtight container in the fridge for up to 3 days.

3 green apples, halved, cored and finely sliced
juice of ½ lemon
500 g baby potatoes
8 radishes, finely sliced
iced water
4 free-range eggs
2 large handfuls watercress
400 g hot-smoked ocean trout fillet, skin removed, flaked
sea salt and freshly ground black pepper
extra virgin olive oil, for drizzling
1 handful mint (optional)

CIDER MAYO
2 free-range egg yolks
1 tablespoon lemon juice
sea salt
125 ml rapeseed oil
2 teaspoons Dijon mustard
2 teaspoons apple cider vinegar
3 tablespoons dry cider
freshly ground white pepper

Serves 4 as a main, 6−8 as a side

Place the apple slices in a bowl and cover with the lemon juice to prevent them from browning. Drain before use.

Place the potatoes in a large saucepan of salted water and bring to a boil. Reduce the heat to medium and simmer for 20−25 minutes or until a knife can be inserted easily into the centres. Drain and set aside to cool, then cut into 1 cm thick slices.

Meanwhile, place the radish slices in a bowl of iced water and leave to stand for 10 minutes to curl slightly, then drain.

Place the eggs in a saucepan, cover with cold water and bring to a boil over high heat. Reduce the heat to medium and simmer for 3 minutes, then plunge the eggs into cold water to halt the cooking process. When cool enough to handle, peel and halve lengthways, then set aside.

For the cider mayo, place the egg yolks, lemon juice and a pinch of salt in the bowl of a food processor. Process on high speed for 1 minute then, with the motor running, add the oil in a thin, steady stream until the mixture is thick and glossy. Add the mustard, vinegar and cider, season to taste with salt and white pepper and process again to combine (makes 240 g).

Toss the apple, potato, radish, egg, watercress and smoked trout together, then stir through the mayo. Season well, drizzle with olive oil and serve garnished with mint, if using.

PROSCIUTTO, FIG AND CHARGRILLED PEACH SALAD

No. 52

For this salad, I like to use San Daniele prosciutto and my favourite blue cheese, the Irish Cashel Blue, which is super-creamy and not too pungent so it won't overpower the other flavours. If watercress isn't in season, use rocket instead.

8 fresh figs, halved lengthways
125 ml light agave nectar (see page 10)
200 g pecans
8 ripe yellow peaches, halved and pitted
light olive oil spray
12 slices prosciutto
200 g good-quality mild, creamy blue cheese, crumbled
1 handful watercress
1 handful mint
sea salt and freshly ground black pepper

SWEET CREAMY DRESSING
100 g creme fraiche
2 teaspoons light agave nectar (see page 10)
juice of 1 small lemon
1 teaspoon Dijon mustard

Serves 8 as a side

Preheat the oven to 200°C/180°C fan/gas 6 and line a baking tray with greaseproof paper.

Place the figs, cut-side up, on the prepared tray. Drizzle with 1 tablespoon of the agave nectar and roast for 7 minutes, then remove and set aside.

Meanwhile, place the pecans in a non-stick frying pan and dry-fry over medium heat for 4–5 minutes, tossing often, until lightly browned. Add 1 tablespoon of the agave nectar and stir through the hot nuts in the pan. Remove and set aside to cool, then slice lengthways.

Spray the flesh-sides of the peaches with olive oil. Combine the remaining agave nectar and 80 ml cold water in a bowl.

Heat a chargrill pan over medium–high heat until almost smoking, then add the peaches in batches, flesh-side down, and cook for 2–3 minutes or until grill marks appear. Turn the peaches over and cook for 1 minute, then carefully spoon some of the agave mixture over the flesh (they will sizzle and spit) and grill for another minute or so. Remove from the pan and cut each half into two or three slices.

For the dressing, whisk all the ingredients together in a small bowl.

To serve, assemble the salad ingredients on a large plate or platter and season to taste. Drizzle a little of the dressing over the top and serve the rest alongside.

NOODLES WITH PRAWNS AND PICKLED CUCUMBER

There are great sweet-and-sour flavours going on in this dish. Don't be nervous about pickling your own cucumber – it's a cinch and once you try it, you'll be hooked. This is a superb summery lunch recipe that tastes great both hot or cold. Nori flakes are available from selected health food stores and Asian food stores.

800 g uncooked prawns, heads removed but tails left intact, deveined
180 g soba noodles
2 long red chillies, seeded and sliced
coriander, to garnish
tamari or light soy sauce, to serve

SOY AND GINGER MARINADE
2 tablespoons tamari or light soy sauce
2 tablespoons brown rice vinegar
1 tablespoon mirin
1 teaspoon fish sauce
1 teaspoon caster sugar
½ teaspoon firmly packed finely grated ginger

PICKLED CUCUMBER
1 tablespoon caster sugar
1 tablespoon black sesame seeds
1 teaspoon nori seaweed flakes
1 cucumber, cut into 1 cm cubes
good pinch of sea salt

Serves 4 as a light lunch

For the marinade, whisk all the ingredients together in a large shallow non-reactive dish. Add the prawns and toss to coat, then cover with cling film and marinate in the fridge for 1 hour.

Meanwhile, for the pickle, combine all the ingredients in a bowl and chill in the fridge for 30 minutes. Taste and add more salt or sugar if desired, then set aside.

Heat a large frying pan or wok over medium–high heat. When hot, add the prawns and the marinade and cook for 2 minutes, turning halfway through, until the prawns are cooked and the sauce has reduced. Remove from the heat and leave to cool completely.

Cook the noodles in a saucepan of simmering water for 3 minutes, then drain and rinse well under cold running water.

Place the noodles, prawns, pickled cucumber and chilli in a bowl and toss to combine. Turn out onto a platter, then drizzle with tamari or soy sauce to taste and garnish with coriander.

QUINOA AND GRAPE SALAD

Champagne grapes are tiny and packed full of sweetness. If you can't find them, use small seedless black grapes or large red grapes cut in half. This colourful salad is always a major crowd-pleaser at barbecues.

190 g red quinoa, rinsed
1 tablespoon olive oil
½ teaspoon ground cinnamon
1 × 400 g tin chickpeas, drained and rinsed
sea salt and freshly ground black pepper
½ small red onion, very finely diced
1 long green chilli, seeded and very finely diced
1 large handful mint, finely chopped, plus extra leaves to garnish
300 g black champagne grapes or 380 g black or red seedless grapes,
    halved or left whole
130 g dried cranberries
160 g almonds, toasted and coarsely chopped
1 tablespoon extra virgin olive oil
finely grated zest and juice of 1 lemon
1 handful baby spinach leaves

Serves 6 as a side

Place the quinoa in a saucepan with 500 ml water and bring to a boil over high heat. Reduce the heat to low and simmer for 25 minutes or until the quinoa is tender and the water has been absorbed. Set aside to cool.

Meanwhile, heat the oil in a large non-stick frying pan over medium heat. Add the cinnamon and stir for 10 seconds. Add the chickpeas, season to taste and stir to coat, then cook for 6–8 minutes, stirring occasionally, until the chickpeas are golden brown and a little crisp – take care as they can spit a little in the oil. Remove from the heat and set aside to cool.

Combine the cooled quinoa and chickpeas in a large bowl, then add the onion, chilli, mint, grapes, cranberries and almonds and stir through.

In a small bowl, whisk together the extra virgin olive oil and lemon zest and add lemon juice to taste. Season with salt, then pour over the salad and toss to coat.

Season and serve with baby spinach and extra mint leaves scattered on top.

PEPPERED BEEF WITH CRISPY NOODLES

When cooking the beef for this dish, I line the frying pan with greaseproof paper, as the sugar in the balsamic burns easily and can ruin your pan in seconds. Use pecorino *sardo* (from Sardinia) or pecorino *toscano* (from Tuscany) if you can find them.

150 g soba noodles
sea salt and freshly ground black pepper
1 tablespoon balsamic vinegar
2 tablespoons extra virgin olive oil, plus extra for drizzling
1 × 400 g free-range beef eye fillet, silver skin removed
(ask your butcher to do this for you)
80 g pine nuts
750 ml rice bran oil
2 large handfuls wild rocket, coarsely chopped
100 g pecorino, shaved
lemon wedges, to serve

Serves 4

Cook the noodles in a saucepan of simmering water for 3 minutes, then drain well. Transfer to sheets of kithen roll to dry thoroughly, blotting away the excess water.

Crush three or four pinches of salt with your fingers onto a plate. Grind 3 teaspoons of pepper onto the plate and mix together.

Place the balsamic vinegar and 1 tablespoon of the olive oil in a bowl. Add the beef fillet and roll it in the liquid, then leave to marinate for 1 minute. Remove the fillet from the liquid, shake off any excess, then coat in the salt and pepper mixture.

Line a frying pan with greaseproof paper, trimming it so it doesn't hang over the edges, and heat over medium–high heat. Add the remaining olive oil and the beef fillet and cook for 6–7 minutes on each side (for medium–rare). Remove from the pan and set aside to rest before slicing finely.

Toast the pine nuts in a frying pan over low–medium heat for 6–7 minutes or until light golden-brown, then set aside.

Heat the rice bran oil in a large, heavy-based saucepan to 180°C. Working in small batches of about a handful at a time, carefully add the noodles (the oil may spit and bubble) and fry for 1 minute. Turn the noodles over with tongs and cook for a further 1–2 minutes or until they are crisp and just golden brown. Remove with a mesh skimmer or a slotted spoon and drain on kitchen roll. When all the noodles have been fried and cooled completely, break them up into small pieces.

To serve, scatter the meat, crispy noodles, pine nuts, rocket and pecorino on a large board or platter. Season well with pepper, then drizzle over some more olive oil and serve with lemon wedges.

FARRO WITH FETA, LEMON AND PINE NUTS

Farro is an Italian wholegrain that's low in gluten. I use
it a lot in salads as it has a great, nutty texture and is very
versatile. I like wholegrain and unpearled varieties: you'll
need to adjust the cooking time if using the cracked or
pearled type. Farro is available from health food stores
and some supermarkets.

250 g wholegrain farro
1 × 250 g punnet cherry tomatoes, quartered
1 long green chilli, very finely chopped
80 g pine nuts, toasted
½ small red onion, very finely chopped
2 cloves garlic, very finely chopped
1 large handful flat-leaf parsley, finely chopped
1 large handful basil, finely chopped, plus extra to garnish
1 large handful mint, finely chopped
1 large handful rocket, finely chopped
200 g feta
finely grated zest and juice of 1 lemon
2 tablespoons extra virgin olive oil
sea salt and freshly ground black pepper

Serves 4 as a side

Place the farro in a saucepan with 500 ml water. Cover and
bring to a boil, then reduce the heat to low and simmer for
30 minutes or until the farro is cooked through. Drain and
rinse well under cold running water, then drain again to
remove as much water as possible.

Place the farro in a large bowl along with the tomato,
chilli, pine nuts, onion, garlic, herbs and rocket. Toss
to combine well, then crumble in half the feta. Add the
lemon zest and juice and the olive oil and season to taste.

To serve, crumble over the remaining feta and garnish
with a few extra basil leaves.

KATIE'S PASTA SALAD

Everybody loves a good pasta salad to serve at a barbecue: this is my version,
jam-packed full of great flavours and colourful textures.

200 g thinly sliced pancetta
500 g small pasta shells
2 cobs sweetcorn, husks and silks removed
1 red onion, finely diced
1 red, 1 yellow and 1 orange pepper, trimmed, seeded and finely diced
1 cucumber, cut into 5 mm dice
1 × 250 g punnet cherry tomatoes, quartered
100 g pitted green olives, thinly sliced
100 g salted capers, well rinsed
80 g pine nuts, toasted
40 g black chia seeds
16 large basil leaves, coarsely chopped
snipped chives, to garnish

DRESSING
3 tablespoons extra virgin olive oil
2 tablespoons apple cider vinegar
½ teaspoon French mustard
sea salt and freshly ground black pepper

Serves 6–8 as a side

Preheat the oven to 200°C/180°C fan/gas 6 and line two baking trays with
greaseproof paper.

Arrange the pancetta on the trays and bake for 12–15 minutes or until crisp. Remove
from the oven and leave to cool slightly before crumbling into small pieces.

Cook the pasta shells according to the packet instructions, then drain and rinse
well under cold running water.

Meanwhile, cook the corn in a saucepan of boiling water for 2–3 minutes, then lift out
with tongs, shake off the excess water and place each cob directly on a gas burner on
medium heat for 1–2 minutes each, turning often, to lightly blacken the kernels. Leave
to cool slightly, then stand the cobs on one end on a board and, using a sharp knife,
carefully slice off all the kernels and place in a large serving bowl.

Place all the salad ingredients (except the chives) into the bowl with the corn
and toss together.

For the dressing, whisk together the oil, vinegar and mustard, then season to taste
and drizzle over the salad. Toss well and serve topped with snipped chives.

COUSCOUS WITH SPICED CHICKPEAS AND POMEGRANATE

This salad pairs brilliantly with any grilled meat, especially lamb.
The pomegranate seeds offer little bursts of fruity flavour, and look
very pretty and jewel like.

200 g couscous
sea salt and freshly ground black pepper
100 g flaked almonds
1 tablespoon olive oil
1 × 400 g tin chickpeas, drained and rinsed
1 teaspoon ground cumin
finely grated zest and juice of 1 lemon
seeds from 2 pomegranates
1 large handful mint, torn
extra virgin olive oil, for drizzling

Serves 4 as a side

Cook the couscous according to the packet instructions. Fluff with a fork
to break up any lumps, then season to taste and set aside in a large bowl.

Toast the flaked almonds in a frying pan over medium heat for 5 minutes or
until golden brown, then set aside to cool.

In the same frying pan, heat the oil over medium heat and add the chickpeas,
cumin and salt and pepper. Cook for 8–10 minutes, tossing often, until crisp
and golden. Add the lemon juice and cook for another minute or two, then
transfer the contents of the pan to the bowl with the couscous, along with the
cooled toasted almonds.

Add the pomegranate seeds, mint, lemon zest and a good drizzle of extra virgin
olive oil and gently toss to combine. Season with a little extra salt and pepper
before serving.

SWEETCORN, BLACK RICE AND CHIA SALAD

Black rice is available from selected health food stores and supermarkets and is a nice alternative to brown rice; if you can't find it, use whichever rice you prefer. This fresh-tasting, punchy salad goes particularly well with Mexican food or barbecued fish or chicken.

200 g black rice
2 cobs sweetcorn, husks and silks removed
1 × 250 g punnet cherry tomatoes, halved
4 spring onions, trimmed and finely sliced
1 large handful flat-leaf parsley
1 large handful mint
1½ tablespoons chia seeds, plus extra to garnish
finely grated zest and juice of 1 large lime
1 tablespoon extra virgin olive oil
sea salt and freshly ground black pepper

Serves 4–6 as a side

Cook the rice according to the packet instructions, then rinse under cold water and drain. Set aside to cool completely.

Meanwhile, cook the corn in a saucepan of boiling water for 2–3 minutes, then lift out with tongs, shake off the excess water and place each cob directly on a gas burner on medium heat for 1–2 minutes each, turning often, to lightly blacken the kernels. Leave to cool slightly, then stand the cobs on one end on a board and, using a sharp knife, carefully slice off all the kernels and place in a large bowl. Set aside to cool completely, then add the tomato, spring onion, herbs and chia seeds.

Whisk together the lime zest, juice and extra virgin olive oil in a small bowl and season to taste. Pour over the salad and gently toss to coat.

Serve garnished with extra chia seeds.

SPICED BUTTERNUT SQUASH AND APPLE SOUP WITH BACON

№ 68

This is an absolute favourite of mine – it's fantastic as a dinner-party starter, and I always get lots of compliments when I serve it. I had never thought about putting apple in a soup before, but it works really well here with the butternut squash and adds just the right amount of sweetness to contrast with the bacon and spices.

50 g pumpkin seeds
1 teaspoon cumin seeds
1 teaspoon coriander seeds
1 teaspoon dried sage
1 kg butternut squash, peeled, seeded and cut into 3 cm pieces
70 ml olive oil
sea salt and freshly ground black pepper
2 green apples, peeled, cored and cut into 3 cm pieces
500 g free-range bacon, fat and rind removed, diced
1 onion, chopped
3 cloves garlic, finely chopped
1 litre chicken stock
120 g goat's cheese

Serves 4

Preheat the oven to 200°C/180°C fan/gas 6 and line two baking trays with greaseproof paper. Scatter the pumpkin seeds on one of the trays and bake for 5 minutes until lightly golden brown.

In a small, non-stick frying pan, toast the cumin and coriander seeds over low heat for 2–3 minutes or until fragrant. Transfer to a mortar, add the sage and grind to a fine powder with the pestle.

Place the butternut squash, ground spices and 2 tablespoons of the oil in a large bowl, season and toss to coat. Tip onto the second tray, arrange in a single layer and roast for 30 minutes. Add the apple and cook for a further 20 minutes or until the butternut squash and apple are tender.

Meanwhile, heat another 2 teaspoons oil in a large frying pan over medium heat. Add the bacon and cook, stirring often, for 5 minutes or until golden. Set aside to drain on kitchen roll.

Heat the remaining oil in the frying pan. Add the onion, garlic and a pinch of salt, then cook, stirring, for 3–4 minutes or until softened. Transfer to a blender along with the butternut squash mixture, 500 ml of the stock, half the goat's cheese and half the bacon, and blend until smooth.

Tip the pureed butternut squash mixture into a large saucepan, add the remaining stock and cook over medium heat for 8–10 minutes or until reduced slightly, then season.

To serve, divide the soup among bowls and sprinkle the remaining bacon and goat's cheese over the top. Finish with a scattering of toasted pumpkin seeds and a grinding of pepper.

CARROT AND GINGER NYC SOUP

When I was in New York for the James Beard Awards in 2013, I booked dinner at the famed Eleven Madison Park. It was to be a sixteen-course degustation(!), so I decided it was best to eat little or nothing that day in preparation for the food-fest that awaited me. By 4 p.m., however, after five hours' shopping downtown, I was starving. I went into a bar in Greenwich Village, got chatting to the owner and she recommended a small bowl of their carrot and ginger soup. It was incredible, and this is my take on it.

6 large carrots, coarsely chopped
½ teaspoon fennel seeds
3 tablespoons olive oil
sea salt and freshly ground black pepper
1 onion, chopped
3 cloves garlic, finely sliced
2 sticks celery, chopped
1 × 3 cm piece ginger, peeled and grated
3 sprigs thyme, leaves stripped, plus extra sprigs to garnish
1.5 litres vegetable stock
sour cream and Walnut Bread (see page 209), to serve

Serves 6

Preheat the oven to 200°C/180°C fan/gas 6 and line two baking trays with greaseproof paper.

Place the carrot, fennel seeds and 2 tablespoons of the oil in a bowl, then season and toss to coat. Tip onto the prepared trays, spread out evenly and roast for 30–40 minutes or until the carrot is tender and starting to caramelise, then remove and set aside.

Heat the remaining oil in a large saucepan over medium heat. Add the onion and garlic and cook, stirring, for 3–4 minutes or until the onion has softened. Add the celery and cook for 3–4 minutes or until softened. Add the ginger, thyme, stock and roasted carrot, bring to a boil, then reduce the heat to low and simmer, stirring occasionally, for 25–30 minutes until thickened. Remove from the heat and blend until smooth with a hand-held blender.

Divide among bowls and top with sour cream, extra thyme sprigs, and a grinding of pepper. Serve with walnut bread.

NEW YORK
HOUSE NUMBER
AND
TRANSIT GUIDE

MAP No. 3000   SIZE: 33"x31"

COMPILED, PRINTED AND PUBLISHED
HAGSTROM COMPANY
MAP MAKERS, PUBLISHERS, LITHOGRAPHERS
20 VESEY STREET   NEW YORK 7, N.Y.

EXPLANATION
Subway Lines (I R T West Side)
Subway Lines (I R T East Side)
Subway Lines (B M T)
Subway, 42nd St. Shuttle
Subway Lines (IND)
Subway Express Stations
Subway Local Stations
Elevated Lines
Elevated Express Stations
Elevated Local Stations
Hudson Tubes
Playgrounds
House Numbers
Surface Lines
Bus Lines
Main Auto Routes

2,350 ETC.

FISH AND CLAM CHOWDER

This recipe was inspired by a chowder I had in Provincetown, Massachusetts, during a trip there a few years ago. I like to use ling or blue-eye, but any meaty white fish would work well.

1 kg clams
1 tablespoon olive oil
250 g free-range bacon, fat and rind removed, cut into batons
1 onion, chopped
2 cloves garlic, finely chopped
2 tablespoons plain flour
1 litre fish stock
5 sprigs thyme, tied in a bunch with kitchen string
1 bay leaf
500 g waxy potatoes, cut into 2–3 cm pieces
sea salt and freshly ground black pepper
250 ml milk
250 ml whipping cream
500 g firm white fish fillets, skin and bones removed,
    cut into 3 cm pieces
finely chopped flat-leaf parsley and crusty bread, to serve

Serves 4–6

Soak the clams in cold water for 30 minutes to remove any grit, then drain, rinse and set aside.

Heat the oil in a large saucepan over medium–high heat. Add the bacon and cook, stirring often, for 3–4 minutes, then add the onion and garlic and cook for 2–3 minutes until softened. Add the flour and stir to coat.

Stir in the stock, thyme, bay leaf and potato and season. Bring to a boil, then reduce the heat to low–medium and simmer for 20 minutes or until the potato is just tender when pierced with a small, sharp knife.

Stir in the milk and cream. Increase the heat to high, add the clams and fish and cook for 3–4 minutes, stirring, until the clams are cooked and the shells are open, and the fish is just cooked.

Serve immediately with plenty of freshly ground black pepper and flat-leaf parsley, accompanied by crusty bread.

ROAST TOMATO, LENTIL AND CHICKPEA SOUP

This is a great winter warmer that's suitable for vegetarians. Feel free to add more harissa if you like things a little more spicy. Serve with plenty of crusty bread.

1.5 kg plum tomatoes, halved lengthways
2 red peppers, trimmed, seeded and each cut into eight wedges
sea salt and freshly ground black pepper
60 ml extra virgin olive oil
1 large red onion, finely chopped
4 large cloves garlic, finely chopped
2 sticks celery, finely sliced
2 long red chillies, seeded and finely chopped
1½ teaspoons harissa
2 × 400 g tins chopped tomatoes
1 teaspoon smoked paprika
½ teaspoon ground cumin
500 ml vegetable stock
2 × 400 g tins lentils, drained and rinsed
2 × 400 g tins chickpeas, drained and rinsed
natural yoghurt and thyme, to serve

Serves 6–8

Preheat the oven to 180°C/160°C fan/gas 4 and line a baking tray with greaseproof paper.

Place the tomato and peppers on the prepared tray, cut-side up, season with salt and drizzle with 2 tablespoons of the oil. Roast for 1 hour or until the tomato is starting to brown at the edges and the peppers are tender. Peel the skin from the peppers once cooked.

Meanwhile, heat the remaining oil in a large heavy-based saucepan over medium heat. Add the onion and cook for 3–4 minutes or until soft, then add the garlic and cook, stirring, for 3–4 minutes or until fragrant. Add the celery and chopped chilli and cook, stirring often, for 4–5 minutes. Stir in the harissa, then add the tinned tomatoes, paprika and cumin and cook for 5–6 minutes.

Remove the pan from the heat, add the roast tomato and capsicum and use a hand-held blender to puree until smooth. Return the pan to medium heat, then add the stock, season to taste and simmer for 10 minutes.

Add the lentils and chickpeas and warm through for 1 minute, then season again. Serve hot with a grinding of pepper, a swirl of yoghurt and some thyme scattered over the top.

In Dublin's
fair city

JOHN JAMESON & SON
ESTABLISHED 1780
JJ&S
PURE POT STILL
DUBLIN WHISKEY.

SPECIAL MEATBALLS

HOMEMADE SOUP
IRISH STEW

RELAX
WITH A
GLASS
OF
WINE

RESTAURANT
OPEN

COFFEE

ESPRESSO	200/220
MACHIATO	220/240
LONG BLACK	240
FLAT WHITE	270
CAPPUCCINO	270
HOT CHOCOLATE	300
TEAS	2

I took a trip back to my hometown of Dublin last year. It had been a while since I'd visited my old stomping ground, and I couldn't wait to catch up with all my mates and my sister and her family. I flew in on my birthday and met up with a big group of friends for cocktails at a funky little bar called Vintage Cocktail Club that's hidden away in the Temple Bar area, before heading to one of my all-time favourite Dublin pubs, McDaids, just off Grafton Street. McDaids is an authentic Dublin pub, buzzing with locals and only a few tourists. The weather was amazing — 30°C and beautifully sunny, a rarity in Dublin — and the city was packed with people, all out enjoying pints of Guinness on the streets.

During my stay, I immersed myself in the burgeoning food scene in Dublin; wowzers, it has totally taken off! Funky, cool new restaurants are popping up all over the city, and they're really hopping all week long. I had a blast shooting loads of pics in some fabulous new spots. Given the economic downturn in Ireland in recent years, it was nice to see things are on the up.

There's a great new chain of urban restaurants by Irish restaurateur John Farrell – his diner-style Dillinger's, The Butcher Grill steakhouse and his amazing Mexican eatery, 777, are all worth a visit if you are in Dublin. Another place I adore is The Fumbally, a funky coffee house that serves delicious salads and sandwiches with a Middle-Eastern feel. This place attracts a young crowd and the food is served in a great space that has a very laidback, creative feel. Mayfield Eatery is another relaxed spot for brunch or dinner. Run by a lovely bloke called Kevin Byrne, it's charming (very shabby-chic), and the food is cosy and warming. It's a little way out of the city, but hop on a bus and you'll be there in no time.

It was amazing being back home for a decent amount of time and seeing all my family and friends. Living on the other side of the globe, I miss them a lot, and the time difference between Sydney and Dublin is a bit of a bummer when it comes to calling each other! I wanted to spend as much time with them as possible, so I arranged plenty of get-togethers at my good friend Colm's house (remember his soup from my first book?). I cooked up some of the recipes from the book and had a great time catching up with my sister and my old school friends, including Emily, Julie, Rebecca and Sarah, not to mention all their gorgeous kids.

When I left Ireland back in 2006, my only niece, Erika, was three years old. She's eleven now, so I've missed a lot of her growing-up years and I relish catching up with her whenever I can. The weather was amazing so we threw a good few barbecues at my sister's place. My brother-in-law, Claudio, is a real character. He's Brazilian and therefore a superman on the barbecue – in fact, he's one of the best on the planet at cooking sausages (the one food I really miss from home – Irish pork sausages are, quite simply, the best in the world!).

Places I visited and websites of interest:

vintagecocktailclub.com
mcdaidsirishpub.com
dillingers.ie
thebutchergrill.ie
777.ie
thefumbally.ie
mayfieldeatery.ie

MENU

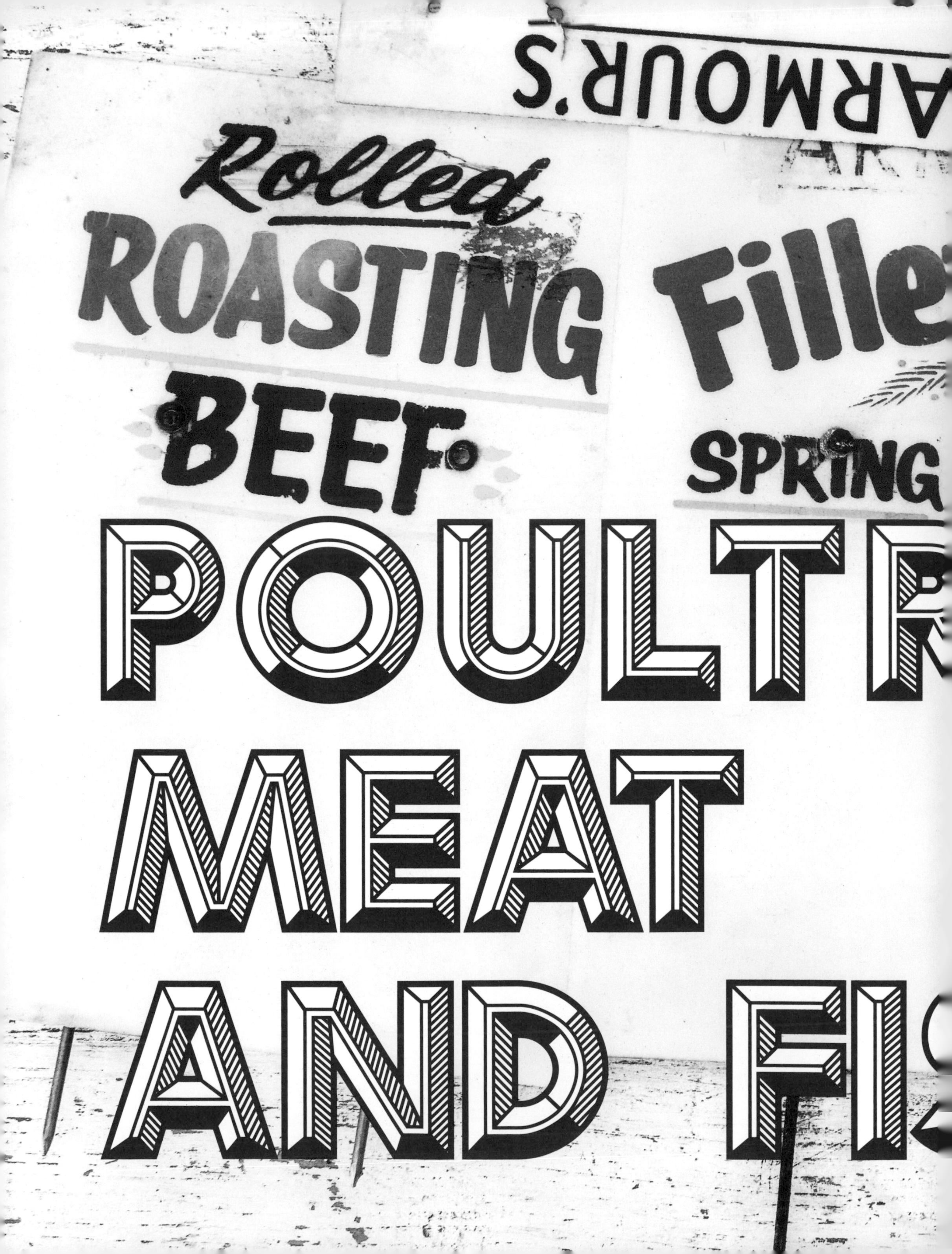

Rolled

ROASTING

Fille

BEEF

SPRING

POULTR

MEAT

AND FIS

ARMOUR'S

TO-DAY PRICE
4/8
PER LB.

ARMOURS

Loins of
SPRING Lamb

S OF
amb
Y.

SH

ARMO

CHICKEN
PORTIONS

179
West
4th St.
NEW YORK
10014

POULTRY, MEAT
AND FISH

№. 90

BUFFALO-INSPIRED WINGS WITH BLUE-CHEESE MAYO

On my first visit to New York in 1997, I visited a bar in Greenwich Village called Down the Hatch, which was (and still is) famous for its 'Atomic Wings' – deep-fried chicken wings smothered in a spicy 'buffalo' sauce (said to originate from the city of Buffalo). I ate buckets of them, and have been hooked ever since – so much so that I've spent years experimenting in the kitchen, trying to perfect my own version of the sauce. Finally, I can present it to you here! A few tips: hot sauce is available from selected gourmet delis and supermarkets. Don't use Tabasco sauce as a substitute as it's too hot for this recipe. Also, don't add the butter to the sauce until right at the end when the pan is off the heat, otherwise the sauce will split.

12 free-range chicken wings
light olive oil spray
1 tablespoon plain flour
1 teaspoon cayenne pepper
1 teaspoon sweet paprika
1 teaspoon onion salt
celery sticks, to serve

BLUE-CHEESE MAYO
3 free-range egg yolks
1 tablespoon white vinegar
2 tablespoons lemon juice
sea salt
250 ml sunflower or rapeseed oil
1 heaped teaspoon Dijon mustard
2 tablespoons light sour cream
150 g blue cheese

BUFFALO-INSPIRED SAUCE
250 ml white vinegar
2 tablespoons honey
2½ tablespoons hot sauce
1 teaspoon sweet paprika
1 teaspoon garlic powder
½ teaspoon cornflour
1 tablespoon lemon juice
1 teaspoon butter

Serves 4–6

Recipe continues overleaf →

BEE
NUT

Thank You!

ON TO SAT
5 TO 1145

SUN
5 TO 11

WEEKENDS
11 TO 230

RRY OUT
AILABLE

Preheat the oven to 200°C/180°C fan/gas 6 and line two baking trays with greaseproof paper.

Remove the tips from the chicken wings, then cut the wings in half at the joint. Pat them dry with kitchen roll, then lightly spray all over with olive oil.

Place the flour, cayenne pepper, paprika and onion salt in a large zip-lock plastic bag, seal and shake to combine. Add the chicken to the bag and shake well to coat evenly in the spice mixture.

Divide the chicken among the prepared trays and bake for 30 minutes. Remove the trays from the oven and use tongs to turn the chicken pieces over (wiping away any excess moisture with kitchen roll), then return the trays to the oven for a further 30 minutes or until the chicken is crisp, golden brown and cooked through.

Meanwhile, for the mayo, place the egg yolks, vinegar, lemon juice and a pinch of salt in the bowl of a food processor. Mix on high speed, adding the oil in a thin, steady stream – you'll end up with a thick, glossy mayo. Add the mustard, sour cream and blue cheese and mix until smooth. Transfer to a serving bowl and chill until required.

For the buffalo-inspired sauce, place the vinegar, honey, hot sauce, paprika, garlic powder and 125 ml water in a saucepan. Bring to a boil, then reduce the heat to medium and simmer for 10–15 minutes. In a small cup, whisk the cornflour with 1 tablespoon water until smooth. Whisk this into the sauce, then simmer, whisking continuously, for 5 minutes. Stir in the lemon juice, reduce the heat to low and cook for 1–2 minutes. Remove the pan from the heat and stir in the butter until it has melted and the sauce is smooth and glossy (don't return the sauce to the heat or it will split).

Place the chicken in a lined serving basket and drizzle with the sauce (keep some parts uncovered so they remain crisp). Serve immediately with the blue-cheese mayo and celery sticks alongside.

NYC

KELLY
I ANG

10
11
12
13
14
15
16
17
18

4
5
6
7
8
9
11
12
13
14
15
16
17
18
19
20
21
22
23

RASPBERRY
ELDERFLOWER
GRANITA

AMERICAN

LIBERTY

201-488-9500

212-986-2121

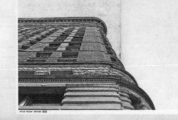

CHILI DOG

Start this dish the day before, if possible, as the chicken is incredibly flavoursome when left to marinate overnight. You can buy pomegranate molasses at Middle-Eastern grocers or selected gourmet delis. If you haven't used it before, you'll soon be hooked. It's sticky and sweet and sour, and pairs fantastically with chicken. Pour it over a roast chicken towards the end of the cooking time and you'll get a great contrast in flavours. It looks superb, too, caramelised on the skin. This dish goes particularly well with the quinoa salad on page 56.

POMEGRANATE CHICKEN

12 free-range skinless chicken thigh fillets, trimmed of excess fat
pomegranate molasses (optional), mint and pomegranate seeds, to serve

POMEGRANATE MOLASSES MARINADE
2 tablespoons olive oil
80 ml pomegranate molasses
juice of 1 lemon
3 large cloves garlic, finely chopped
2 tablespoons Dijon mustard
2 tablespoons sherry vinegar
2 sprigs mint, leaves picked and very finely chopped
sea salt and freshly ground black pepper

Serves 4–6

For the marinade, place all the ingredients in a jug or bowl and whisk to combine. Pour into a large zip-lock plastic bag, add the chicken thighs, then seal and shake to combine. Marinate in the fridge for at least 6 hours (or overnight if possible).

Heat a chargrill pan or barbecue flat plate over medium– high heat until hot. Working in batches, cook the chicken thighs for 5–6 minutes on each side until golden brown and cooked through.

Drizzle over some pomegranate molasses, if using, then serve hot, scattered with mint and pomegranate seeds.

CRUNCHY CHICKEN WITH SWEET-SALTY DIPPING SAUCE

This dish is a healthy choice, and kids will love it, too. Tamari (Japanese soy sauce) is available from Asian food stores, delis and most supermarkets.

8 free-range skinless chicken thigh fillets, trimmed of excess fat
3 tablespoons tamari
3 tablespoons light agave nectar (see page 10)
20 g puffed quinoa
75 g rolled quinoa flakes
105 g black or white sesame seeds (or a mixture of both)
freshly ground black pepper

SWEET—SALTY DIPPING SAUCE
4 tablespoons tamari
2 tablespoons light agave nectar (see page 10)
2 tablespoons mirin
1 long red chilli, seeded and finely sliced
2–3 spring onions, trimmed and finely sliced
2 cloves garlic, very finely chopped
few sprigs coriander

Serves 4

Halve the chicken thighs lengthways. Place the tamari and agave nectar in a small shallow dish and whisk together. Add the chicken and toss to coat, then cover with cling film and refrigerate for 1 hour.

Preheat the oven to 200°C/180°C fan/gas 6 and line two baking trays with greaseproof paper.

Place the puffed quinoa, quinoa flakes, sesame seeds and a good pinch of black pepper in a large bowl and combine. Remove the marinated chicken from the fridge and, working one by one, take a piece of chicken from the marinade, allowing the excess to drip off, then place in the bowl and toss to coat with the quinoa mixture. Transfer to the prepared trays.

Bake the chicken for 20–25 minutes or until golden, crispy and cooked through.

Meanwhile, for the dipping sauce, place the tamari, agave nectar, mirin and 1 tablespoon water in a jug and whisk to combine. Pour into a small serving bowl and stir in the chilli, spring onion, garlic and coriander.

Serve the hot chicken strips with the dipping sauce alongside.

GRILLED CHICKEN WITH LIME AND HERBS

You'll need about 160 ml lime juice for this recipe, so if fresh limes are out of season and too expensive, you could use bottled lime juice instead.

6 limes, plus extra wedges to serve
2 tablespoons olive oil
1 long green chilli, seeded and finely chopped
1 handful mint, finely chopped, plus extra leaves to garnish
1 handful coriander, finely chopped, plus extra sprigs to garnish
sea salt and freshly ground black pepper
12 free-range skinless chicken thigh fillets, trimmed of excess fat
finely sliced green chilli, to garnish

Serves 6

Finely grate the zest of two of the limes into a large shallow glass or ceramic bowl. Add the juice from all six limes, reserving the squeezed lime halves, then stir in the oil, chilli and herbs. Season.

Add the chicken and turn to coat in the marinade. Scatter the squeezed lime halves on top, then cover and marinate in the fridge for at least 3–4 hours.

Before cooking, bring the chicken to room temperature.

Heat a chargrill pan or barbecue flat plate over medium–high heat. Working in batches if necessary, use a pair of tongs to transfer the chicken pieces to the hot grill, draining off any excess marinade as you go. Cook, turning occasionally, for 10–12 minutes or until lightly charred and cooked through.

Serve immediately with extra sliced chilli, mint, coriander and lime wedges.

CRISPY CHICKEN TACOS

This fried chicken is so delicious you may have a hard time getting it into the tortillas: you'll want to snaffle it straight away instead. If you're pushed for time, use a bought ranch-style dressing for the slaw rather than making your own mayo. Hot sauce is available from selected gourmet delis and most supermarkets.

600 g free-range skinless chicken thigh fillets,
    trimmed of excess fat, halved lengthways
180 ml buttermilk
1–2 teaspoons Tabasco sauce
sea salt
2 cobs sweetcorn, husks and silks removed
1 long green chilli, finely chopped
freshly ground black pepper
100 g rice flour
75 g plain flour
rice bran oil, for deep-frying
8 corn tortillas
lime juice, hot sauce or chipotle sauce (see page 28)
    and coriander, to serve

CREAMY SLAW
1 free-range egg yolk
1¾ tablespoons lemon juice
sea salt
100 ml rapeseed oil
2 teaspoons Dijon mustard
1 teaspoon white wine vinegar
2 tablespoons light sour cream
200 g red cabbage, very finely sliced
200 g white cabbage, very finely sliced
1 carrot, peeled and finely grated (you'll
    need about 150 g grated carrot)

Serves 4

Place the chicken thighs in a bowl and add the buttermilk, Tabasco and a good pinch of salt. Using clean hands, mix everything together to coat the chicken thoroughly. Cover with cling film and marinate in the fridge for 1–2 hours.

Meanwhile, for the slaw, place the egg yolk, 1 tablespoon lemon juice and a pinch of salt in the bowl of a food processor. Process on high speed, adding the oil in a thin, steady stream until the mixture is thick and glossy. Add the mustard, vinegar and sour cream and process again to incorporate. Transfer to a bowl, cover with cling film and place in the fridge.

Cook the corn cobs in a saucepan of boiling water for 2–3 minutes, then lift out with tongs, shake off the excess water and place each cob directly on a gas burner on medium heat for 1–2 minutes each, turning often, to lightly blacken the kernels. Leave to cool slightly, then stand the cobs on one end on a board and, using a sharp knife, carefully slice off all the kernels. Place in a bowl, add the chilli and stir to combine, then season to taste.

Combine the flours in a bowl. Remove the chicken from the marinade, shake off any excess and dredge in the flour.

Quarter-fill a large, heavy-based saucepan with oil. Heat over high heat until the temperature reaches 180°C, then reduce the heat to medium–high. Working in batches of about eight pieces at a time, fry the chicken for 4 minutes, turning once or twice, until golden brown, crispy and cooked through. Drain on kitchen roll, patting off the excess oil, then transfer to a plate, season with plenty of sea salt and cover with foil.

Heat a chargrill or frying pan over high heat and toast a tortilla on both sides until lightly browned. Transfer to a plate and cover with foil to keep warm, then continue with the remaining tortillas.

For the slaw, toss the cabbage and grated carrot together in a bowl, then add half the dressing and the remaining lemon juice and toss to combine.

To serve, add some slaw and corn to the middle of a warm tortilla and top with crispy chicken. Add a squeeze of lime juice and a splash or two of sauce, then drizzle over a little of the remaining slaw dressing. Finish with a scattering of coriander.

ROAST CHICKEN WITH BACON, KALE AND ALMOND STUFFING

This is one of my staple quick and easy dinner-party recipes: I cooked it at my Barossa lunch (see pages 32–41) and it went down a treat. I absolutely adore stuffing, so I always make extra and serve it alongside the bird. You can have it in sandwiches the following day, too.

1 onion, roughly chopped

3 cloves garlic, peeled

50 g almonds

1 handful flat-leaf parsley

2 sprigs rosemary, leaves stripped and chopped

150 g sourdough bread, crusts removed

250 g free-range bacon, fat and rind removed, finely diced

130 g curly kale, stalks removed, leaves finely sliced

1–2 pieces preserved lemon rind, rinsed and diced

1 apple, grated

sea salt and freshly ground black pepper

1 × 1.5 kg free-range chicken

40 g unsalted butter, softened

1 tablespoon olive oil

2–3 lemons, halved or quartered and a few sprigs rosemary (optional)

Serves 4

Preheat the oven to 200°C/180°C fan/gas 6.

Place the onion and garlic in a food processor and whiz until finely chopped but not mushy, then transfer to a large bowl. Whiz the almonds in the food processor until medium–finely chopped, then add to the bowl. Add the herbs to the processor and whiz until finely chopped, then add to the bowl. Finally, whiz the bread in the processor to fine breadcrumbs and place in the bowl.

Add the bacon, kale, preserved lemon and apple to the bowl, season with pepper and combine well. Set aside.

Carefully separate the skin from the chicken breasts, taking care not to tear the skin. Slide half the butter under the skin of each breast, then carefully spread the butter out evenly by rubbing your fingers over the top of the skin.

Season the cavity of the chicken. Take two handfuls of the stuffing mix and form into a loose ball. Push into the cavity, taking care not to overstuff the bird, then tie the legs together with kitchen string to help hold the stuffing in place. Pop the remaining stuffing on a sheet of foil, form it into a sausage shape and roll up to secure.

Place the chicken in a roasting tin, season with salt and pepper and drizzle with the oil. Tuck the lemons and rosemary, if using, around the chicken and roast for 30 minutes, then place the foil-wrapped stuffing in the oven and cook for a further 40 minutes or until the chicken is cooked through and the skin is crisp and golden brown.

Set the chicken aside to rest for 10 minutes before carving and serving with the extra stuffing alongside.

INDIAN-SPICED LAMB CUTLETS

These cutlets are fantastic to serve at a barbecue or casual dinner party; they are wonderfully flavoursome and always get snapped up quickly. I usually allow four cutlets per person as they are so popular. Serve them on a platter and let people help themselves. They go really well with the couscous and chickpea salad on page 65 and the smashed baby potatoes on page 160. Start this the day before if you have time, as the lamb is even more delicious if left to marinate overnight.

16 free-range lamb cutlets, French-trimmed (ask your butcher to do this for you)
lemon wedges, to serve

INDIAN-SPICED MARINADE
80 ml olive oil
3 teaspoons garam masala
1 teaspoon ground cumin
1 teaspoon dried oregano
3 large cloves garlic, finely chopped
1 handful flat-leaf parsley, very finely chopped
1 handful mint, very finely chopped
finely grated zest and juice of 1 large lemon
sea salt and freshly ground black pepper

Serves 4

For the marinade, place all the ingredients in a jug or bowl, season with salt and pepper and whisk to combine. Pour into a large zip-lock plastic bag with the lamb cutlets, seal and shake to combine.

Marinate in the fridge for at least 6 hours (or overnight if possible).

Heat a chargrill pan or barbecue flat plate over medium–high heat until hot. Working in batches, cook the cutlets for 2 minutes each side for medium–rare, then serve hot with lemon wedges.

LAMB SHANK PIE

A total winner for a winter dinner party, this is a joy to prepare and is guaranteed to impress! This pie goes perfectly with the mashed potato on page 166. I use a gutsy red wine for this: a cab sav/shiraz blend is ideal.

Serves 6–8

35 g plain flour
8 × 300 g free-range lamb shanks, trimmed of excess fat
2 tablespoons rice bran oil
2 brown onions, quartered
2 carrots, cut into 2 cm thick rounds
3 sticks celery, diced
8 large cloves garlic, peeled
1 × 750 ml bottle good-quality red wine
6 sprigs rosemary, leaves stripped from 4 of the sprigs
4 sprigs thyme, leaves stripped
750 ml beef stock
1 tablespoon tomato puree
2 tablespoons Worcestershire sauce
1 tablespoon Dijon mustard
sea salt and freshly ground black pepper
finely grated zest of 1 large lemon
1 sheet good-quality puff pastry
1 free-range egg yolk mixed with a little milk

Preheat the oven to 155°C/135°C fan/gas 2.

Place the flour on a large plate, add the shanks and toss to coat.

Heat the oil in a large flameproof casserole over medium–high heat. Working in batches, brown the shanks evenly on all sides, then remove and drain on kitchen roll.

Arrange the onion, carrot, celery and garlic in the casserole. Place the lamb shanks on top, pour over three-quarters of the red wine (reserving the rest to drink) and scatter over the rosemary and thyme leaves.

Place the stock, tomato puree, Worcestershire sauce and mustard in a large bowl or jug, whisk together and season with salt and pepper. Pour this mixture over the shanks, then add the lemon zest. Place the lid on the casserole and bake for 4–5 hours or until the lamb is very tender.

Remove the casserole from the oven. Transfer the lamb shanks to a large bowl and set aside until cool enough to handle. Strip the meat from the bones – it should come away easily – and transfer to a clean bowl. Reserve six or seven of the bones, rinse them well under cold water and set aside.

Transfer the meat to a 3 litre capacity pie dish, and spoon in the cooked vegetables from the casserole using a slotted spoon. Mix well and check for seasoning.

Spoon off any excess fat from the liquid in the casserole, then place over medium–high heat. Bring to a boil, then reduce the heat to medium and simmer for 25–30 minutes or until the sauce has reduced by almost two-thirds and is thick and glossy.

Preheat the oven to 210°C/190°C fan/gas 6. Pour the sauce over the ingredients in the pie dish. Carefully lay the pastry sheet on top and pinch to seal the edges. Using a small sharp knife, pierce six or seven holes in the pastry and insert the cleaned shank bones. Brush the pastry with eggwash.

Bake for 35–40 minutes or until the pastry is puffed and golden brown. Serve piping hot.

SPICED LAMB WITH LEMON

Saturday afternoon barbecue? Sorted. This dish is perfect for a large gathering, as you can cook two or three lamb legs, slice them up and pop it all on a platter. Serve this with the farro salad on page 60 (you could even put out pita breads as well and fill them with the meat and salad — no plates required!).

8 cardamom pods
1 tablespoon coriander seeds
1 tablespoon fennel seeds
1 teaspoon ground cinnamon
sea salt and freshly ground black pepper
finely grated zest of 1 lemon, plus an extra 2 lemons, quartered lengthways, pips removed
4 large cloves garlic, roughly chopped
180 ml extra virgin olive oil
1 x 1.5 kg free-range boneless leg of lamb, butterflied

Serves 6

Bruise the cardamom pods with the back of a knife, extract the seeds and place them in a small, non-stick frying pan along with the coriander and fennel seeds. Toast over low—medium heat for 2 minutes or until fragrant.

Transfer the toasted spices to a mortar along with the cinnamon and 1 teaspoon each of salt and pepper. Grind with a pestle to a fine powder. Add the lemon zest, garlic and olive oil, then mix together to form a paste.

Place the lamb in a large shallow dish and use your hands to thoroughly massage the marinade into the meat. Cover and marinate in the fridge for 4 hours.

Once the lamb has been marinating for 3 hours, preheat the oven to 200°C/180°C/gas 6.

Place the lemon quarters on a baking tray lined with greaseproof paper and roast in the oven for 1 hour. Remove and set aside.

Heat a barbecue or chargrill pan to high. Remove the lamb from the fridge and place on the grill, cooking for 5—6 minutes on both sides for medium—rare.

Set the meat aside to rest for 15 minutes before slicing.

Serve the sliced lamb on a platter lined with greaseproof paper, surrounded by roasted lemons and sprinkled with sea salt.

CHORIZO AND TOMATO TART

During my last visit back home to Dublin, I found the most incredibly pretty and colourful heirloom tomatoes in a gourmet food shop. I took them home and created this dish with some chorizo I had in the fridge, a huge bunch of basil, a box of oh-so-pretty micro herbs and a bottle of aged balsamic. Super-simple and very pretty to serve at a summery weekend brunch or as a starter.

1 sheet good-quality puff pastry
1 free-range egg yolk mixed with a little milk
220 g good-quality chorizo sausages, thinly sliced
8–10 (400 g) tomatoes, sliced
sea salt and freshly ground black pepper
80 ml extra virgin olive oil
1 small handful basil, plus extra to garnish (optional)
micro herbs and flowers, to garnish (optional)

Serves 4 for a light brunch

Preheat the oven to 200°C/180°C fan/gas 6 and line a baking tray with greaseproof paper.

Lay the pastry sheet on the prepared tray and brush with eggwash. Using a small, sharp knife, score a 1.5 cm border around the edge of the pastry sheet, taking care not to cut right through the pastry. Prick the centre of the pastry sheet a few times with a fork. Place a folded 20 cm square of greaseproof paper in the middle of the pastry and gently weigh down with a small saucepan lid.

Blind-bake for 20 minutes, then remove the tray from the oven. Remove the weight and greaseproof paper, then line the pastry with the chorizo and the sliced tomato, overlapping slightly if you need to. Season with a little salt and pepper and drizzle over 1 tablespoon oil, then bake for 25–30 minutes or until the pastry is puffed around the edges and golden brown.

Meanwhile, blend the basil and the remaining oil to a smooth paste, then season to taste.

To serve, drizzle the basil oil over the tart and garnish with extra basil or micro herbs and flowers, if using.

PORK FLAUTAS WITH CREAMY APPLE AND RADISH SLAW

These deep-fried filled and rolled tortillas are not for the faint-hearted, but are wonderful to feed a hungry crowd. Make sure to reserve half the dressing from the slaw, as it's great to dip the flautas into. Serve them immediately after frying so they stay crisp.

2 teaspoons coriander seeds
1 teaspoon caraway seeds
2 teaspoons garlic powder
1 teaspoon sea salt
1 teaspoon sweet paprika
1 teaspoon ground cinnamon
2 teaspoons cocoa powder
1 teaspoon dried chilli flakes
1 teaspoon onion powder
125 ml chipotle sauce (see page 28)
60 ml olive oil
1 x 2 kg free-range pork shoulder, bone in
2 brown onions, quartered
6 large cloves garlic, skin-on
1 carrot, cut into 2 cm rounds
500 ml apple cider
10-12 corn tortillas
rice bran oil or olive oil, for shallow frying

CREAMY APPLE AND RADISH SLAW
1 tablespoon apple cider vinegar
150 g good-quality mayo
60 g sour cream
finely grated zest and juice of 1 lemon
200 g red cabbage, very finely sliced
8 radishes, trimmed and very finely sliced using a mandoline
1 green apple, cored and cut into thin matchsticks, then covered in a squeeze of lemon juice
1 handful coriander leaves

Serves 4–8

Preheat the oven to 160°C/140°C fan/gas 3.

Place the coriander and caraway seeds in a small, non-stick frying pan over low–medium heat and toast until fragrant. Add to a mortar along with the garlic powder, salt, paprika, cinnamon, cocoa powder, chilli flakes and onion powder and grind with a pestle to a fine powder. Transfer to a large roasting tin, add the chipotle sauce and oil and combine well. Add the pork, and use your hands to thoroughly massage the marinade into the meat.

Arrange the onion, garlic cloves and carrot around the pork in the roasting tin. Pour the cider into the tin, along with 250 ml water, transfer to the oven and roast uncovered for 4½ hours, checking every now and then to ensure the liquid does not evaporate (add a little more water at any point if the tin looks dry).

Allow the pork to cool for 15 minutes before transferring to a chopping board and shredding the meat from the bone with two forks. Remove the cooked vegetables from the tin with a slotted spoon and discard, then place the shredded meat back in the tin and toss to coat in the sauce.

Preheat the oven to 150°C/130°C fan/gas 2. Lay the tortillas out on a clean surface. Divide the shredded pork among the tortillas, arranging it in a line across the centre. Roll up into a tube and secure with a toothpick.

Fill a large heavy-based frying pan with oil to a depth of 1 cm and heat to 160–170°C. Working in batches of two or three, fry the flautas for 1–2 minutes each side until golden brown and super-crispy, then remove and drain briefly on kitchen roll. Keep the fried flautas warm in the oven while you cook the rest.

For the slaw, combine the vinegar, mayo, sour cream, lemon zest and juice in a small bowl. Place the cabbage, radish and apple in a large bowl, add half the dressing and toss well to combine. Scatter over the coriander.

Remove the toothpicks from the fried flautas and cut them in half crossways. Serve with plenty of slaw and the remaining slaw dressing to the side.

POULTRY, MEAT
AND FISH

No. 117

MONTHLY

WEEKLY

WEEKLY

CHIPOTLE, LIME AND JALAPENO RIBS

This is one of my favourite recipes in the book, due to my current adoration of anything containing chipotle! These are sticky and sweet and spicy and sour — a great option to cook up on a weekend and serve with cold beers.

1.5 kg free-range baby back pork ribs
250 ml chipotle sauce (see page 28)
250 ml light agave nectar (see page 10)
finely grated zest of 4 limes
250 ml lime juice
3 jalapeno chillies, seeded and finely sliced
sea salt
lime wedges and coriander, to garnish

Serves 4

Preheat the oven to 200°C/180°C fan/gas 6.

Bring a large saucepan of water to a boil, then add the ribs and simmer for 30 minutes, skimming off any fat from the surface from time to time.

Whisk together the chipotle sauce, agave nectar, lime zest and juice, chilli and a good pinch of salt in a bowl until combined.

Place the ribs in a baking dish, cover with the sauce and roast for 15 minutes. Reduce the oven temperature to 170°C/150°C fan/gas 3 and roast for a further 1–1¼ hours, basting well every 15 minutes, or until the sauce is thick, glossy and caramelised.

Serve hot with lime wedges to the side and coriander scattered on top.

ROAST PORK WITH CIDER AND MAPLE SYRUP

Years ago, my mum introduced me to the art of stuffing and roasting a pork fillet, and I've been doing this for dinner parties and Sunday lunches ever since. As I mentioned earlier, I'm a huge fan of stuffing, so I always make extra and serve it alongside the pork, or save it for sandwiches the next day.

2 × 400 g free-range pork tenderloin fillets
sea salt and freshly ground black pepper
60 ml maple syrup
2 tablespoons olive oil
750 ml dry cider
250 ml single cream

PRUNE AND APPLE STUFFING
1 brown onion, finely chopped
4 large cloves garlic, finely chopped
150 g pitted prunes, finely chopped
100 g macadamias, toasted and roughly chopped
100 g fresh breadcrumbs
2 green apples, grated
1 handful flat-leaf parsley, finely chopped
8–10 sage leaves, finely chopped
5 sprigs thyme, leaves stripped
sea salt and freshly ground black pepper

Serves 4

Preheat the oven to 210°C/190°C fan/gas 6.

For the stuffing, place all the ingredients in a bowl and combine well.

Lay the pork fillets on a clean surface. Season the insides well, then arrange one-third of the stuffing on one of the fillets. Top with the second fillet, seasoned-side down, and secure with kitchen string at 3 cm intervals. Pop the remaining stuffing on a sheet of foil, form it into a sausage shape, roll up to secure and set aside.

Place the stuffed fillet on a roasting rack set over a roasting tin.

Whisk together the maple syrup, oil and half the cider in a small bowl, then pour over the meat. Roast for 50 minutes–1 hour or until the pork is cooked through and caramelised, placing the foil-wrapped stuffing in the oven after 25 minutes. Remove the pork to a plate and cover to keep warm, and set the stuffing aside.

Place the roasting tin containing the juices on the hob over high heat and add the remaining cider. Simmer for 10–12 minutes or until the liquid has reduced by one-third. Whisk in the cream and simmer for 3–4 minutes or until the gravy is nice and thick.

Cut the pork into thick slices and serve with the cider gravy and extra stuffing to the side.

SLOW-ROASTED PORK RAGU

A wonderful, cosy meal to enjoy with a good bottle of red. If you have time to make your own pasta, so much the better, but I find I always resort to buying fresh or dried pasta for this.

2 onions, quartered
1 head garlic, cloves separated and peeled
1 × 750 ml bottle good-quality red wine
1 × 1.5 kg free-range pork shoulder, bone in
olive oil, for drizzling
sea salt and freshly ground black pepper
8 large plum tomatoes, halved
1 large handful basil
2 × 400 g tins chopped tomatoes
1 tablespoon balsamic vinegar
1 tablespoon finely grated lemon zest
2 tablespoons chopped oregano
600 g pappardelle or tagliatelle
grated parmesan, to serve (optional)

Serves 6–8

Preheat the oven to 160°C/140°C fan/gas 3.

Scatter the onion and garlic in a large roasting tin, then pour over half the wine and 250 ml water. Set a roasting rack over the tin and place the pork on the rack. Drizzle the pork with 1 tablespoon oil, then season well. Roast for 3 hours, checking every now and then and adding a splash of water if the tin looks dry.

At the 3-hour mark, put the tomato halves into a baking dish, then season and drizzle with 1 tablespoon oil. Place in the oven with the pork and roast for 2 hours until the tomato is soft and starting to collapse and the pork is tender (remember to keep checking from time to time that the roasting tin is not drying out).

Remove the pork and tomato from the oven. Transfer the pork to a chopping board and set aside, then spoon the onion, garlic and juices from the roasting tin into a blender, along with the tomato halves and their juices. Add the basil and blend to a smooth sauce.

Place the blended sauce in a large saucepan and add the tinned tomatoes, vinegar, lemon zest, oregano and remaining wine. Season and simmer over low–medium heat for 45 minutes or until thickened.

Meanwhile, shred the pork, discarding the skin, fat and bones, and set aside.

Cook the pasta according to the packet instructions, then drain.

Add the meat to the sauce in the pan and cook for 10 minutes or until the meat has warmed through and the sauce thickens a bit more.

Add the pasta to the sauce and stir to combine. Divide among serving bowls and serve with plenty of freshly ground black pepper and grated parmesan, if using.

SMOKY BEEF CHILLI WITH BLACK BEANS

I am super-proud of this recipe: it took me months of fine-tuning, and it's smoky and sweet and totally yum. It's definitely worth the effort! You'll find dried ancho and chipotle chillies at gourmet delis. I use Jack Daniels sour mash bourbon for this, but another brand would work just as well.

2 large dried ancho chillies
2 dried chipotle chillies
boiling water, for soaking
1 kg free-range beef chuck, trimmed of excess fat,
    cut into 3 cm cubes
2 tablespoons plain flour
sea salt and freshly ground black pepper
4 tablespoons olive oil
1 brown onion, diced
4 cloves garlic, finely chopped
2 teaspoons ground cumin
2 teaspoons smoked paprika
1 teaspoon ground cinnamon
1 teaspoon dried oregano
1 tablespoon cocoa powder

1 litre beef stock
80 ml bourbon
1 tablespoon chipotle sauce (see page 28)
1 bay leaf
2 red peppers, trimmed, seeded and
    cut into bite-sized pieces
2 × 400 g tins chopped tomatoes
2 tablespoons tomato puree
2 tablespoons muscovado or dark brown sugar
1 × 400 g tin black beans, drained and rinsed
1 × 400 g tin kidney beans, drained and rinsed
coriander, to garnish
steamed brown rice, sour cream and grated cheese, to serve

Serves 6–8

Place the dried chillies in a heatproof jug, cover with boiling water and set aside for 30 minutes to reconstitute. Drain, then finely chop, reserving the seeds, and set aside.

Place the beef and flour in a large zip-lock plastic bag, season and shake well to coat evenly.

Heat 1 tablespoon oil over medium heat in a large, heavy-based casserole, add half the beef and brown on all sides for 2–3 minutes. Remove to a plate lined with kitchen roll, then repeat with another tablespoon of oil and the remaining beef.

Add another tablespoon of oil to the casserole and cook the onion and garlic over medium heat for 3–4 minutes or until the onion is soft. Stir in the spices and oregano and cook for 1 minute, stirring constantly.

In a small cup, whisk together the cocoa and 2 tablespoons beef stock, then add this mixture to the dish along with the remaining stock, the bourbon, chipotle sauce, bay leaf, red peppers, tomatoes, tomato puree, sugar, the reserved beef and chopped chilli and seeds. Stir well to combine, then partially cover with the lid and bring to a boil. Reduce the heat to low and simmer for 1½ hours or until the beef is very tender, checking and stirring every 15 minutes or so to make sure the mixture doesn't catch on the bottom of the casserole.

Add the beans and simmer for a further 15 minutes. Season and serve garnished with coriander, with steamed rice, sour cream and grated cheese to the side.

BEEF WELLINGTON

A classic dish that pairs perfectly with my creamy indulgent mash on page 166 and loads of good hearty shiraz. There's enough batter here to make around seven crepes, which is more than you'll need but allows for some mistakes!

50 g plain flour
1 free-range egg
250 ml milk
2 teaspoons finely chopped flat-leaf parsley
1 teaspoon finely chopped thyme,
    plus extra sprigs to garnish
sea salt and freshly ground black pepper
olive oil, for cooking
1 × 850 g free-range beef eye fillet, silver skin removed
    (ask your butcher to do this for you)

1 tablespoon Dijon mustard
1 tablespoon horseradish cream
1 sprig rosemary, leaves stripped and
    very finely chopped
40 g butter
300 g chestnut mushrooms, finely chopped
6 large slices prosciutto
1 large sheet good-quality puff pastry
1 free-range egg yolk mixed with a little milk

Serves 4–6

Sift the flour into a mixing bowl and make a well in the centre. Crack in the egg and whisk into the flour, then gradually pour in the milk, whisking until the batter is smooth. Stir in the herbs and season.

Heat a non-stick 20 cm crepe or frying pan over medium heat, then add enough oil to just coat the base of the pan. Add 2½ tablespoons batter and swirl the pan so the batter coats the base evenly. Cook for 1–2 minutes until golden, then flip with a spatula and cook on the other side for 30 seconds–1 minute until golden. Transfer to a plate and repeat with the remaining batter until you have four uniformly round crepes.

Heat 2 tablespoons oil in a frying pan and sear the beef fillet on all sides until browned, then set aside. Mix 1 tablespoon each of salt and pepper together on a plate. Combine the mustard, horseradish cream and rosemary in a small bowl. Use a knife to spread this paste all over the seared beef, then roll the fillet in the salt and pepper mixture.

Wipe the pan clean, then place it over medium heat and melt the butter. Add the mushrooms and a pinch of salt and cook for 12–15 minutes or until most of the moisture has evaporated. Remove the mushrooms from the pan and set them aside to cool completely.

Lay the prosciutto slices lengthways on a large piece of greaseproof paper, overlapping them slightly. Spread the mushrooms evenly over the prosciutto, leaving a 3 cm

border. Place the beef fillet on top crossways, and bring the overhanging prosciutto up and over to cover the meat and mushrooms securely.

On another large piece of greaseproof paper, lay the four crepes in a square pattern, overlapping by 1–2 cm, then place the prosciutto-wrapped fillet on top and use the greaseproof paper to bring the crepes up and over to cover the fillet completely. Peel off the greaseproof paper.

Finally, lay the puff pastry sheet on another piece of greaseproof paper and roll out to 30 cm square. Place the crepe parcel in the centre. Moisten the edges of the pastry with water to create a good seal. Fold one side of the pastry over the beef, tuck the ends in, then roll the parcel over so it is fully enclosed in the pastry. Press the edges together well, then place on a plate, seam-side down, and chill in the fridge for 15 minutes.

Preheat the oven to 200°C/180°C fan/gas 6 and place a baking tray inside to heat.

Brush the pastry with eggwash, then lift the greaseproof paper and the pastry parcel onto the heated tray and bake for about 40 minutes or until the pastry is golden and the meat is cooked to your liking (if using a meat thermometer, the temperature will register 55°C for medium–rare).

Set aside to rest for 5 minutes before cutting into 2–3 cm slices and serving.

THE 'MANWICH'

A sure-fire way to please your man, or anyone with a healthy appetite, for that matter.
Any leftover beer and onion jam is perfect served as part of a cheese platter alongside
a strong cheddar. For the pesto, you can use ordinary kale leaves with the central stems
removed if you can't get hold of baby kale.

sea salt and freshly ground black pepper
2 × 220 g free-range sirloin steaks
8 thick slices crusty bread
1 large clove garlic, halved
30 g baby spinach leaves
2 vine-ripened tomatoes, sliced
150 g good-quality mayo,
mixed with 3 teaspoons barbecue sauce (optional)

BEER AND ONION JAM
1 tablespoon olive oil
2 large red onions, halved and finely sliced
sea salt
2 tablespoons firmly packed brown sugar
125 ml beer
2 tablespoons balsamic vinegar

SPINACH AND KALE PESTO
50 g baby spinach leaves
50 g baby kale leaves
30 g walnuts
60 g goat's cheese

Serves 4

For the jam, heat the oil in a large non-stick frying pan over medium heat. Add the onion and a good pinch of salt and cook, stirring often, for 10–12 minutes or until the onion is starting to caramelise. Stir in the sugar, beer and vinegar and cook, stirring often, over low–medium heat for a further 15 minutes or until the jam is thick and glossy. Remove from the heat and set aside.

For the pesto, place all the ingredients in a food processor and blitz to a thick, smooth paste (adding a teaspoon or so of water to loosen if needed).

Season the steaks well on both sides. Heat a barbecue grill plate or chargrill pan to medium–high and cook the steaks for 3–4 minutes on each side or until cooked to your liking. Transfer to a plate and set aside to rest for 5–6 minutes, then cut into 2 cm thick slices.

Grill the bread until lightly toasted, then rub one side with the cut garlic.

Spread half the bread slices with pesto, then add a small handful of spinach leaves, some sliced tomato, some sliced steak and a dollop of onion jam. Top with barbecue mayo, if using, then add the bread lids and serve held together with a skewer.

TRUFFLE BEEF BURGERS WITH CREAMY MUSHROOMS AND PANCETTA

№ 130

Truffle salt is expensive, but you only need a small amount and a little goes a long way. You'll find it at selected gourmet delis.

2 tablespoons olive oil

300 g Swiss brown mushrooms, 100 g chopped, 200 g thickly sliced

3 sprigs thyme, leaves stripped

800 g lean minced free-range beef

1 small brown onion, finely chopped

4 large cloves garlic, finely chopped

½ teaspoon truffle salt

70 g parmesan, finely grated

3 teaspoons tomato puree

1 teaspoon Dijon mustard

sea salt and freshly ground black pepper

8 thin slices pancetta

3 tablespoons creme fraiche

thinly sliced vintage cheddar, lettuce leaves and sliced tomato, to serve

4 white burger rolls or brioche buns

Serves 4

Heat 1 tablespoon oil in a large non-stick frying pan over medium heat. Add the chopped mushrooms and thyme and cook, stirring, for 2–3 minutes or until browned, then transfer to a bowl and set aside to cool.

Place the mince, onion, garlic, truffle salt, parmesan, tomato puree, mustard, salt and pepper in a large bowl. Using clean hands, mix everything together well. Shape into four patties about 11 cm in diameter and place on a plate lined with kitchen roll. Cover with cling film and refrigerate for 30 minutes.

Preheat the oven to 200°C/180°C fan/gas 6 and line two baking trays with greaseproof paper.

Spread out the pancetta on one of the prepared trays and bake for 6–10 minutes or until crisp and browned.

Preheat a barbecue grill plate or chargrill pan until hot. Cook the burgers for 2–3 minutes on each side, then

transfer them to the remaining tray, place in the oven and cook for 6–8 minutes or until done to your liking. Remove them from the oven and set them aside to rest for 10 minutes.

Meanwhile, heat the remaining oil in a large non-stick frying pan over high heat. Add the sliced mushrooms and cook for 3–4 minutes until softened and browned. Remove the pan from the heat and stir through the creme fraiche, then season to taste and transfer to a serving bowl.

Top each burger with some reserved mushroom and thyme mixture and a slice or two of cheese, then pop under the oven grill briefly to melt the cheese.

To assemble, place some lettuce, sliced tomato and pancetta on each bun base. Top with the mushroom and cheese-topped burger, then finish with the bun lid and serve with creamy mushrooms alongside.

CHILLI AND TAMARIND PRAWN CURRY

Tamarind puree is readily available in jars, but for a fresher tamarind flavour you can prepare your own using tamarind pulp. Place 1 tablespoon pulp in a small saucepan with 60 ml water and bring to a simmer over medium–high heat. Once simmering, cook for 30 seconds–1 minute, breaking up with a potato masher, until the pulp has dissolved and the liquid has thickened slightly. Push through a fine-mesh sieve with the back of a spoon, discarding the seeds and fibre, and use the resulting puree in the recipe. Both the pulp and puree are available from Asian food stores.

- 2 tablespoons olive oil
- 2 small brown onions, finely chopped
- 5 large cloves garlic, finely chopped
- sea salt and freshly ground black pepper
- 2 long green chillies, seeded and finely chopped,
  plus extra sliced chilli to garnish
- 2 × 400 g tins chopped tomatoes
- 750 ml chicken stock
- 2 tablespoons fish sauce
- 1 stalk lemongrass, white part only, finely chopped
- 2 kaffir lime leaves, very finely shredded
- 4 spring onions, finely sliced
- 1 tablespoon tamarind puree
- 1 × 400 ml tin coconut milk
- 1 kg uncooked tiger prawns, peeled and deveined
- 1 large handful coriander, finely chopped,
  plus extra leaves to garnish
- finely grated zest and juice of 2 small limes,
  plus extra lime wedges to serve
- steamed rice, to serve

Serves 4

Heat the oil in a large saucepan over medium heat. Add the onion, garlic and a pinch of salt and cook, stirring, for 4–5 minutes or until the onion is soft. Add the chilli, tomato, stock, fish sauce, lemongrass, kaffir lime leaves, spring onion, tamarind and coconut milk and stir to combine. Simmer for 20 minutes.

Stir in the prawns and coriander, then season and cook for a further 2–3 minutes or until the prawns are just cooked. Stir in the lime zest and juice and garnish with extra chilli and coriander. Serve with steamed rice and lime wedges.

SEA TROUT WITH LEMON AND CHAMPAGNE SAUCE

This is a simple dish with wonderful, subtle flavours. A good one for a celebration dinner, it goes well with boiled and minted baby potatoes.

1 × 750 ml bottle dry white wine
2 sticks celery, finely sliced
1 small bulb fennel, trimmed and finely sliced, fronds reserved and roughly chopped
1 teaspoon black peppercorns
2 lemons, finely sliced, pips removed
1 bunch tarragon, 12 leaves finely chopped and set aside for the sauce, remaining leaves stripped
1 tablespoon salted capers, well rinsed
1 × 1 kg side sea trout, skin-on and pin-boned (ask your fishmonger to do this for you)
lemon thyme, to serve
freshly ground black pepper

LEMON AND CHAMPAGNE SAUCE
1 free-range egg yolk
1 teaspoon white wine vinegar
1 tablespoon lemon juice
sea salt and freshly ground white pepper
250 ml sunflower oil
1 teaspoon Dijon mustard

80 ml sparkling wine or champagne

Serves 6

Pour the wine and 2.5 litres water into a large roasting tin (mine is 26 cm ×x 36 cm ×x 8 cm), then add the celery, fennel, fennel fronds, peppercorns, lemon slices, tarragon leaves and capers. Place over medium–high heat and bring to a boil, then reduce the heat to medium and simmer for 10–12 minutes.

Add the fish, skin-side down, and simmer for 5 minutes, spooning the liquid over the fish now and then (if the fish protrudes out of the water, push it back down so it is immersed in liquid). Turn off the heat and leave the fish to stand in the water for a further 10 minutes; it will continue to cook in this time.

Meanwhile, for the sauce, place the egg yolk, vinegar, lemon juice and a pinch of salt in the bowl of a food processor. Mix on high speed, adding the oil in a thin, steady stream – you'll end up with a thick, glossy mayo. Add the mustard, some white pepper and the reserved finely chopped tarragon leaves and mix. Pour in the wine or champagne and mix briefly to combine so the mixture is light and creamy. (Makes 450 g.)

To serve, carefully remove the poached fish using two spatulas and place on a serving platter. Scatter the lemon thyme over the fish and grind over some pepper. Serve with the sauce drizzled on top.

FISH TACOS WITH BLACK QUINOA AND SWEETCORN SALSA

I make these a lot for weeknight meals, but they are also fab to take to a weekend picnic. Just make up all the elements in advance, pop them into plastic containers and assemble in situ. Try to get corn tortillas, rather than those made from flour, as they are amazing with the sweetcorn salsa. Tip: never salt the water when boiling corn as it will toughen it.

600 g firm white fish, skin and bones removed,
    cut into 2–3 cm cubes
2 tablespoons extra virgin olive oil
3 limes, plus extra wedges to serve
sea salt and freshly ground black pepper
95 g black quinoa
2 cobs sweetcorn, husks and silks removed
1 × 250 g punnet cherry tomatoes, quartered
4 spring onions, finely sliced
½ small red onion, finely chopped
2 jalapeno or long green chillies, seeded and
    finely chopped
1 large handful mint
1 large handful coriander
200 g sour cream
12 corn tortillas (20 cm diameter), warmed

Serves 4

Place the fish and 1 tablespoon oil in a non-reactive bowl. Add the finely grated zest of one lime and the juice of two limes. Season well, cover with cling film and marinate in the fridge for 1 hour.

Meanwhile, place the quinoa in a saucepan with 1 cup (250 ml) cold water. Bring to a boil, then reduce the heat to low–medium, cover and simmer, stirring occasionally, for 30 minutes or until the quinoa is cooked and the water has been absorbed. Set aside to cool.

Cook the corn in a saucepan of boiling water for 2–3 minutes, then lift out with tongs, shake off the excess water and place each cob directly on a gas burner on medium heat for 1–2 minutes each, turning often, to lightly blacken the kernels. Leave to cool slightly, then stand the cobs on one end on a board and, using a sharp knife, carefully slice off all the kernels and place in a bowl. Once cooled completely, add the tomato, spring onion, red onion and chilli, then squeeze in the juice of half

a lime and leave to stand for 30 minutes to allow the flavours to develop.

Finely chop one-third of the mint and coriander and add to the salsa. Season well and stir to combine, then set aside.

Combine the sour cream and the juice from the remaining half a lime in a small bowl and set aside.

Roughly chop the remaining herbs (leaving a little for the garnish) and place in a bowl. Drain the fish, then toss through the herbs to coat. Heat the remaining oil in a large non-stick frying pan over medium–high heat. Cook the fish, turning, for 1–2 minutes until just cooked and starting to fall apart.

Spread a little lime-flavoured sour cream over each tortilla, then top with quinoa, salsa and fish. Garnish with the remaining herbs and serve with lime wedges.

CHIA-SEED QUICHE WITH TROUT AND POTATO

This is a great 'mother-in-law is coming for lunch on Saturday' dish. You can use bought sour-cream or shortcrust pastry if you are short of time. Micro herbs are available from supermarkets and come in many varieties: baby sorrel would go particularly well with the trout.

400 g baby potatoes, scrubbed
1 tablespoon olive oil
275 g white cabbage, very finely sliced
6 free-range eggs
125 ml milk
120 g creme fraiche, whisked to soften
1 handful dill, snipped into small lengths
2 tablespoons chia seeds
sea salt and freshly ground black pepper
1 × 200 g smoked trout fillet, skin and
    bones removed, flaked
1 handful micro herbs (optional)
green salad, to serve

CHIA SOUR-CREAM PASTRY
270 g plain flour, plus extra for dusting
150 g unsalted butter, chilled and cubed
sea salt
80 g sour cream
2 tablespoons chia seeds

Serves 6–8

For the pastry, place the flour, butter and ½ teaspoon salt in the bowl of a food processor and whiz until it resembles breadcrumbs. Add the sour cream and chia seeds and whiz until the dough just starts to come together; it should be soft and a little sticky to the touch.

Turn the dough out onto a lightly floured surface and press together, shaping into a disc. Wrap in cling film and refrigerate for 30 minutes.

Meanwhile, place the potatoes in a large saucepan of salted water and bring to a boil. Reduce the heat to medium and simmer for 20–25 minutes or until a knife can be inserted easily into the centres. Drain and set aside to cool, then cut into 1 cm thick slices.

Preheat the oven to 200°C/180°C fan/gas 6 and grease a 28 cm diameter loose-based fluted tart tin.

Heat the oil in a deep frying pan over medium–high heat. Add the cabbage and cook, stirring often, for 3–4 minutes or until it's starting to soften and turn golden brown around the edges. Remove from the heat and set aside.

On a floured surface, roll out the pastry to a thickness of 5 mm and use to line the prepared tin, patching any holes that may appear. Refrigerate the pastry case for 30 minutes.

Take two large pieces of greaseproof paper and scrunch them up in your hands, then smooth them out and use to line the pastry case, overlapping them to cover the whole base. Fill with baking beans or rice and blind-bake for 20 minutes, then remove the paper and beans or rice and bake for a further 12–15 minutes or until the pastry is light golden. Set aside to cool.

Whisk together the eggs, milk, creme fraiche, dill and chia seeds and season with salt and pepper.

To assemble the quiche, line the pastry with the sliced potato, then cover with cabbage and scatter the flaked trout on top. Carefully pour in the egg mixture, lightly pressing down on the ingredients to let the liquid come to the top. Bake for 30–35 minutes or until golden brown and cooked through.

Serve hot or at room temperature scattered with micro herbs, if using, and a green salad to the side.

STUFFED ROAST SNAPPER

You can make this dish using a whole red snapper but I find it easier to use two large fillets; make sure to ask your fishmonger to pin-bone them for you. The stuffing is simple, but works brilliantly due to the contrasting flavours from the salty bacon and sour capers.

olive or rice bran oil, for cooking
2 large golden shallots, finely chopped
2 cloves garlic, finely chopped
250 g free-range bacon, fat and rind removed, diced
1½ tablespoons salted capers, well rinsed
1 small bunch dill, finely chopped, plus extra sprigs to garnish
sea salt and freshly ground black pepper
2 large snapper fillets (about 700 g each), skin removed and pin-boned
2 lemons, quartered

Serves 4–6

Preheat the oven to 210°C/190°C fan/gas 6 and line a baking tray with greaseproof paper.

Heat 1 tablespoon oil in a frying pan over medium heat, add the shallot and cook, stirring often, for 2–3 minutes. Add the garlic and cook, stirring, for 2 minutes, then add the bacon and cook for a further 2 minutes or until the bacon is cooked. Set aside to cool, then tip into a bowl and stir in the capers, dill, salt and pepper.

Season the underside of each fillet with salt. Place one fillet, salted-side up, on the prepared tray. Spoon the stuffing onto the fillet, patting it down well, then top with the second fillet and secure well with kitchen string. Season well, arrange the lemon quarters around the fish and roast for 30–35 minutes or until the fish is just cooked through.

Serve immediately with dill sprigs alongside.

TRATTORIA PIZ

RISTORANTE

ROBERTO

OSTARIA

GELATI ICE CREAM

VILLA SAN DONNINO

E

VIGNOLA
CAMPIGLIO
13
TAVERNELLE

ITALIA!

BOLOGNA

VENICE

CAPRI

Ravello

POSITANO

IL PODESTÀ

DELLA COMUNE DI MODENA

AVVISO.

L. F. MONTECUCCOLI.

TARDINI.

2561 2562 256

stop 1 V E N I C E

stop 2 BOLOGNA

In my mind, Italy is one of the most magical places on this planet. Despite the 24+ hour journey to get there from Sydney, it's a place I fall in love with more and more each time I visit. The people, the landscapes, the history, the medieval towns, the language – I am smitten by it all, but in particular, the food, as well-noted over the years on my blog.

Italian food is my favourite of all cuisines, and I love exploring all the regional cooking styles. Ergo, for my most recent vacation, rather than head back to my regular haunts of Siena and Tuscany, I decided to travel north to Venice and then on to Bologna to savour the culinary wonders this part of the country is famed for: parmesan cheese, cured meat, pork dishes and the most amazing balsamic vinegars I have ever tasted.

I started in Venice, a magical city I feel everyone should visit at least once in their lifetime. I'll never forget seeing the city for the first time on the super-fun water taxi ride from the airport, pinching myself that I was actually there – in Venice! – and marvelling at how utterly bizarre it is to see a city floating on the water. My parents used to have a painting of Venice hanging in our family home that I would gaze at for hours, and now, finally, I had made it here in the flesh!

Visiting Italy in July is always going to mean a lot – note, a LOT – of tourists, so admittedly Venice was jam-packed with people, but it was wonderful to see the men in their striped tops paddling gondolas down the canals, ferrying around tourists who were all manically snapping away at everything with their cameras. I chose to splurge a bit on this trip and booked one of the most beautiful hotels in this fairytale-like city: the famed Gritti Palace. It was divine and offered a romantic view of the Grand Canal and across the water to Santa Maria della Salute; enjoying dinner there by candlelight is a memory I will savour for many years to come.

Next stop: Bologna. What an incredible city, which sadly is often overlooked by visitors to Italy. I was a little underwhelmed initially, but when night fell, this university town came to life. I loved it! It's not half as touristy or expensive as Venice, and I got a very chilled and relaxed vibe from the town.

I decided to book myself on a food tour to get the best out of the city, the home of ragu alla bolognese. After the somewhat rude awakening of having to rise at 6 a.m. (on my holiday!), I was picked up at the hotel by a driver and joined seventeen others for an incredible day spent visiting a parmesan factory, prosciutto manufacturer and, best of all as I adore the stuff, an authentic Modena-based family-run boutique balsamic vinegar business. This was the highlight of my trip and even inspired me to fork out a few hundred dollars for a 100-year-old bottle of balsamic, which I bring out for special dinner parties at home. I learnt how 99 per cent of most balsamic vinegars – even the ones you see in gourmet shops for over $100 per bottle – are not, in fact, 'proper' balsamic, as the real stuff must be bottled in the authentic Modena balsamic bottle, and must only contain 100 per cent pure grape must, without any additional ingredients.

The tour company was a hubby-and-wife set-up; the host, Alessandro, was crazy passionate, extremely knowledgeable and witty. He guided us expertly through a jam-packed, yet leisurely day – the highlight of which was a big group lunch where the food and wine flowed. Take it from me, a food tour is a must if you visit this area.

continued overleaf...

From there I headed south to check out Capri and the Amalfi Coast, a place I had long heard about but never seen. After the fastest, scariest train ride/ rocket journey in my life (no kidding, I think we hit 400 kilometres per hour at one point), I found myself in Naples in all its crazy glory. Sadly, however, it was just for a few hours (I will be back with my camera as the photo ops looked abundant), as then it was straight onto a ferry to Capri.

Oh. My. God. Did someone say nirvana? Capri is stunning. I felt like I was in a James Bond movie; it was so colourful and incredibly pretty. I took the cable car up the hill to Piazza Umberto, the little town square located in the historic centre of Capri. Buzzing with people (all dressed in obligatory white) and the odd glamorous wedding, I was in awe of its beauty. I made my way up the narrow, winding white-walled streets, passing enormous Capri lemons tied in bunches outside shops, to find the hotel where I'd be staying for the next two nights; the uber-stylish Capri Tiberio Palace. It was very chic, and sparked my current obsession with hand-painted patterned tiles – they adorned the balcony of my room and I am now totally obsessed with them! A little further afield, I discovered the quieter and even more beautiful Anacapri, my favourite part of the island. It is a photographer's dream, with abundant bright pink and purple flowers cascading down chalky white walls.

Of all the amazing places I visited on this trip, the one that stood out over all the rest was Positano, the most picturesque village nestled in a bay south of Naples, where the buildings look as though they've been stacked higgledy-piggledy, one above the other, rising up the hillside. I met a Canadian woman there who said she's been back every year for the past twelve years, and I can understand why. As I sat on the ferry approaching Positano from Capri, I must have taken 1,985 photos as the boat pulled into the harbour. Never in my life have I seen such outstanding beauty. The various bright colours of the buildings crammed together climbing up the hill are utterly glorious.

Places I stayed and websites of interest:

thegrittipalace.com
italiandays.it
capritiberiopalace.it
palazzoravizza.it
sirenuse.it

LA
MELAGRANA

CERAMICHE S. RUBINO ANACAPRI

LE SIREN
HOTEL

POSITANO

SPICED CAULIFLOWER CHEESE WITH CRUNCHY TOPPING

This makes a great weeknight vegetarian meal. Serve it with crusty bread, a green salad and a glass of gutsy red wine.

1 kg cauliflower, broken into florets
1 teaspoon cumin seeds
1 teaspoon coriander seeds
1 tablespoon black sesame seeds
1 tablespoon white sesame seeds
2 tablespoons chia seeds
sea salt and freshly ground black pepper
2 tablespoons olive oil
150 g coarse fresh breadcrumbs, mixed with a little olive oil
1 handful very finely chopped flat-leaf parsley
80 g grated cheddar

CHEESE SAUCE
75 g unsalted butter
60 g plain flour
850 ml milk
170 g grated cheddar
sea salt and freshly ground white pepper

Serves 2 as a main, 6 as a side

Preheat the oven to 200°C/180°C fan/gas 6.

Place the cauliflower in a large saucepan of water and bring to a boil over high heat. Reduce the heat to medium and simmer for 5–6 minutes or until a knife can just be inserted into the florets. Drain well and set aside to cool.

Place the cumin and coriander seeds in a small frying pan over medium heat and fry for 1–2 minutes or until lightly toasted. Transfer to a mortar and grind to a fine powder, then place in a medium-sized baking dish along with the sesame seeds and half the chia seeds. Season with salt and pepper, then add the olive oil and cauliflower and toss to coat.

For the cheese sauce, melt the butter in a large saucepan over medium–high heat. Add the flour and combine with a wooden spoon to form a thick paste. Reduce the heat to low–medium, then gradually add the milk, whisking well between each addition to incorporate and remove any lumps. Add the cheese and stir until melted and smooth, then season well and pour over the cauliflower in the baking dish.

Combine the breadcrumbs, parsley, remaining chia seeds and 40 g of the cheese in a bowl, then scatter this mixture over the cauliflower. Top with the remaining cheese and season. Bake for 20–25 minutes or until the top is golden brown and crisp. Serve hot.

SMASHED POTATOES WITH ROSEMARY

These are easy to cook and always get eagerly gobbled up: I recommend making double the amount, as they disappear fast. They go really well with the lamb cutlets on page 106, along with, quite frankly, almost anything else.

1.5 kg baby potatoes, scrubbed, larger ones cut in half widthways
125 ml rice bran oil
4–5 sprigs rosemary, leaves stripped
sea salt and freshly ground black pepper

Serves 4 as a side

Preheat the oven to 210°C/190°C fan/gas 6.

Place the potatoes in a large saucepan of salted boiling water and bring to a boil. Reduce the heat to medium and simmer for 6–7 minutes or until the potatoes are just starting to soften but are still firm in the middle.

Meanwhile, drizzle the oil into a large non-stick roasting tin and place in the oven for 5–6 minutes to heat up.

Drain the potatoes well, then carefully transfer them to the tin. Scatter over the rosemary and roast for 20 minutes.

Remove the tin from the oven and smash each potato firmly with the back of a spoon. Sprinkle over some sea salt, then return the tin to the oven for a further 25–30 minutes or until the potatoes are golden brown and super-crispy. Season with pepper and serve immediately.

CELERIAC AND POTATO GRATIN

If you're looking for the best comfort-food dish ever, then you've found it. Okay, this is not going to get you into those skinny jeans anytime soon, but it's out-of-this-world good. I make it all the time for cosy dinner parties, usually paired with roast lamb. I use a mandoline to cut the potato and celeriac into very fine slices.

600 ml whipping cream
1 heaped teaspoon hot English mustard
1 kg potatoes, very finely sliced
550 g celeriac, peeled and very finely sliced
3 large cloves garlic, very finely sliced
60 g butter
sea salt and freshly ground black pepper
5 small sprigs rosemary
200 g gruyere cheese, coarsely grated, plus an extra handful to scatter

Serves 6 as a side

Preheat the oven to 200°C/180°C fan/gas 6.

Whisk together the cream and mustard in a jug to combine.

Layer one-quarter of the sliced potato in a large baking dish, slightly overlapping the slices. Repeat with one-quarter of the sliced celeriac, then dot with a few slices of garlic and one-quarter of the butter. Season with salt and pepper. Pour over one-quarter of the cream mixture, and scatter with the leaves from a sprig of rosemary and one-quarter of the grated cheese. Repeat this process three more times.

Scatter the top with the extra grated gruyere and remaining rosemary leaves and bake for 45–50 minutes or until the potatoes and celeriac are cooked through and the top is golden brown and bubbling.

ROAST VEGETABLES WITH GOAT'S CURD AND HAZELNUTS

№ 164

A colourful, textural salad that is sure to impress. Use goat's cheese in place of goat's curd if you like.

1 bunch each baby purple and golden beetroot (approximately 6 beetroot per bunch),
    stalks trimmed leaving about 2 cm attached
olive or rice bran oil, for cooking
sea salt and freshly ground black pepper
1 bunch baby carrots, stalks trimmed leaving about 2 cm attached,
    scrubbed and halved lengthways (keep smaller ones whole)
1 tablespoon dry white wine
2 teaspoons unsalted butter
2 sprigs thyme, leaves stripped, plus extra sprigs to garnish
140 g hazelnuts
200 g green beans, trimmed and cut into thin slices lengthways
200 g goat's curd, crumbled
1 tablespoon extra virgin olive oil
1 tablespoon balsamic vinegar

Serves 4 as a side

Preheat the oven to 210°C/190°C fan/gas 6.

Scrub the beetroot clean, then pat dry with kitchen roll and place on a large sheet of foil. Drizzle with oil and sprinkle with a little salt. Wrap up the foil to cover the beetroot and roast on a baking tray for 45 minutes or until tender when pierced with a small sharp knife (the cooking time will depend on the size and freshness of the beetroot; start checking them after about 25 minutes). Set aside to cool.

Meanwhile, lay a sheet of foil on a baking tray and place the carrots on top. Drizzle with oil and add the white wine, butter, thyme leaves, salt and pepper. Cover with a second sheet of foil and pinch the edges to seal. Roast for 20–25 minutes or until tender, then set aside to cool.

Scatter the hazelnuts on a baking tray and roast for 6–8 minutes or until golden brown. Wrap the hot nuts in a clean tea towel and rub to remove the skins. Leave to cool, then crush lightly using a mortar and pestle and set aside.

Cook the beans in a saucepan of boiling salted water for 1–2 minutes or until al dente, then drain and set aside.

Peel the skins from the beetroot, then halve and combine in a large dish with the carrots, beans and goat's curd. Scatter the hazelnuts and a few extra thyme sprigs on top.

Whisk together the oil and vinegar and drizzle over the salad, then season and serve.

KATIE'S PARIS-STYLE MASH

I included a recipe for mash in my first book, but this is the one
I make more regularly nowadays. You will need a potato ricer
and a drum sieve to make the mash silky smooth, although
a fine-mesh sieve will work, too. You want to be really sure there
is no firmness in the middle of the potatoes when boiling them
for mash. If they're not tender right the way through, you'll
struggle to get a super-creamy, lump-free mash.

  1 kg large floury potatoes, unpeeled
  250 ml whipping cream
  60 ml milk
  200 g unsalted butter, plus extra to serve
  sea salt and freshly ground white pepper

Serves 4–6 as a side

Place the potatoes in a large saucepan of salted water and bring to
a boil. Reduce the heat to medium and simmer for 30–40 minutes
or until a knife can easily be inserted into the centre.

Drain well, then leave to dry for 2 minutes before peeling
(use a clean tea towel or rubber gloves to protect your hands).
Return to the dry saucepan and place over low heat for 1–2 minutes,
stirring occasionally, to remove any excess moisture.

Heat the cream and milk in a small saucepan over low heat until
the mixture has warmed through – don't let it boil.

Using a potato masher, partially break up the potatoes. Push them
through a potato ricer on the finest setting then, using the back of
a spoon, push the mash through a drum sieve. When the mash is
smooth and completely lump-free, place it back in the pan over low
heat, then add the warmed milk mixture and beat in lightly with
a wooden spoon. Add the butter and beat lightly until melted and
the mash is piping hot.

Season with salt and a good pinch of ground white pepper,
then add an extra knob of butter, if using, and serve.

SWEET POTATO AND CAULIFLOWER CURRY

A fantastically warming and hearty vegetarian dish with a bit of kick. Look for Malaysian curry powder at Asian food stores; it makes a world of difference to the end result.

1 teaspoon fennel seeds
1 teaspoon coriander seeds
1 teaspoon cumin seeds
½ teaspoon ground turmeric
1 teaspoon Malaysian curry powder
sea salt and freshly ground black pepper
2 tablespoons olive oil or rice bran oil
1 brown onion, finely chopped
4 large cloves garlic, finely chopped
1 long red chilli, seeded and finely chopped
2 tablespoons tomato puree
2 × 400 g tins chopped tomatoes
500 ml vegetable stock
750 g sweet potato, peeled and cut into 2 cm cubes
½ head cauliflower, broken into florets
2 × 400 g tins brown lentils, drained and rinsed
150 g cashews, toasted and coarsely chopped
steamed brown rice, natural yoghurt and coriander, to serve

Serves 6

Place the fennel, coriander and cumin seeds in a non-stick frying pan over medium heat and cook, stirring, for 1–2 minutes or until fragrant. Transfer to a mortar, then add the turmeric, curry powder and a large pinch of salt and pepper and grind to a fine powder with the pestle.

Heat the oil in a large heavy-based saucepan over medium heat. Add the onion and a pinch of salt and cook, stirring often, for 3–4 minutes until softened. Add the garlic and cook for 3 minutes, stirring frequently to avoid burning. Stir in the ground spice mixture and chilli and cook for 2–3 minutes, then stir in the tomato puree, tomatoes and stock. Add the sweet potato and bring to a boil over high heat. Reduce the heat to low, cover and simmer for 25–30 minutes or until the potato is just soft in the centre.

Add the cauliflower florets, stir and continue to cook for 8 minutes, then add the lentils and cook just long enough to warm them through.

Season and serve piping hot with the cashews alongside, as well as steamed brown rice, natural yoghurt and coriander.

MUSHROOM, GOAT'S CHEESE AND PECAN RISOTTO

I love making risottos – they are superb for dinner parties, as you can par-cook them, then finish off the cooking with the last few ladlefuls of hot stock just before serving.

20 g unsalted butter
400 g Swiss brown mushrooms, quartered
1 handful thyme
60 g pecans, halved lengthways
1.25 litres vegetable stock
1 tablespoon olive oil
1 brown onion, finely chopped
3 cloves garlic, finely chopped
400 g arborio rice
250 ml dry white wine
120 g soft goat's cheese
80 g finely grated parmesan, plus extra to serve (optional)
juice of 1 small lemon
60 g rocket leaves, roughly chopped
sea salt and freshly ground black pepper
micro herbs (optional), to garnish

Serves 6–8

Melt the butter in a frying pan over medium–high heat. Add the mushrooms and fry for 2 minutes or until just starting to brown, then add the thyme and cook for 1–2 minutes, stirring often. Remove the pan from the heat and set aside.

Preheat the oven to 200°C/180°C fan/gas 6 and line a baking tray with greaseproof paper.

Scatter the pecans on the prepared tray and roast for 6–7 minutes or until lightly browned, then remove and set aside.

Pour the stock into a saucepan and bring to a simmer over medium heat. Reduce the heat to low, then cover and keep the stock warm until needed.

Meanwhile, heat the oil in a large heavy-based saucepan or flameproof casserole over medium heat. Add the onion and cook, stirring often, for 4–5 minutes or until softened, then add the garlic and cook, stirring often, for 3–4 minutes or until the garlic is lightly golden.

Add the rice and stir to coat, then cook, stirring constantly, for 1–2 minutes or until the rice is lightly toasted. Add the wine to deglaze the pan, then simmer for 1 minute.

Reduce the heat to low–medium and add the hot stock, a ladleful at a time, stirring after each addition until the liquid is almost completely absorbed before adding the next. Continue until all the stock has been added and the rice is al dente (it should take around 20 minutes), stirring constantly and ensuring the rice does not dry out (you can add water if you run out of stock).

Add the mushrooms, pecans, goat's cheese, parmesan, lemon juice and rocket and stir to combine. Season with salt and pepper, then serve with extra parmesan and micro herbs, if using.

THREE-BEAN POTATO PIE

If you don't have a flameproof casserole, you can make the filling for this pie
in a large saucepan, then transfer it to a lightly greased 2½ litre capacity
pie dish before baking.

1 tablespoon olive oil
1 brown onion, finely chopped
3 large cloves garlic, finely chopped
1 carrot, finely chopped
2 sticks celery, finely chopped
1 leek, white part only, trimmed, washed and finely sliced
1 long red chilli, seeded and finely diced
1 teaspoon smoked paprika
1 tablespoon tomato puree
60 ml red wine
250 ml vegetable stock
1 handful each basil and oregano, torn
sea salt and freshly ground black pepper
750 g sweet potato, peeled and cut into 3 cm cubes
550 g floury potatoes, cut into 3 cm cubes
30 g unsalted butter
60 ml whipping cream
1 × 400 g tin adzuki beans, drained and rinsed
1 × 400 g tin borlotti beans, drained and rinsed
1 × 400 g tin kidney beans, drained and rinsed
200 g baby spinach leaves
80 g finely grated parmesan, plus extra to serve
toasted pumpkin seeds, to serve

Serves 6

Heat the oil in a large flameproof casserole over medium heat. Add the onion and garlic and cook for 4–5 minutes, stirring often, or until softened. Add the carrot, celery, leek and chilli and cook, stirring often, for 4–5 minutes or until the vegetables have softened. Stir in the paprika and tomato puree to coat, then add the red wine, stock and herbs, season to taste and cook over low–medium heat for 15–20 minutes or until the sauce has thickened slightly.

Preheat the oven to 200°C/180°C fan/gas 6.

Meanwhile, place the sweet potato and potato in a large saucepan of salted water and bring to a boil. Reduce the heat to medium and simmer for 12–15 minutes or until

a knife can easily be inserted into the centre. Drain well, then return them to the pan and mash. Add the butter and cream and stir to combine, then season to taste, cover and set aside.

Add the beans and baby spinach to the casserole and stir to combine well. Simmer for 2 minutes or until the spinach has just wilted and beans are warmed through, stirring regularly. Season to taste, then spoon the mash on top and fluff up with a fork. Scatter with parmesan, transfer to the oven and bake for 20–25 minutes or until golden brown.

Serve piping hot with toasted pumpkin seeds and extra grated parmesan scattered over the top.

BABY AUBERGINE WITH HARISSA AND GARLIC

Super-easy, super-quick, super-tasty! These are little pops of flavour that make a fantastic side dish (especially with lamb), or nibbles for a dinner party.

1½ teaspoons harissa
2 tablespoons olive oil
2 large cloves garlic, finely chopped
500 g baby aubergines, cut into thick rounds
sea salt
1 small handful mint, finely chopped
freshly ground black pepper

Serves 4 as a side

Preheat the oven to 200°C/180°C fan/gas 6 and line a baking tray with greaseproof paper.

Place the harissa, oil and garlic in a large shallow dish and combine. Add the aubergine and toss to coat well, then transfer to the prepared tray.

Season well with salt and roast for 20–25 minutes or until tender. Scatter with chopped mint and season with pepper before serving.

MUSHROOM AND CARAMELISED ONION QUESADILLAS

Quesadillas are brilliant for get-togethers. I often cook up a bunch of fillings and let people assemble their own before sticking the filled tortillas in the pan and warming them through.

2 tablespoons olive oil
2 onions, sliced
3 teaspoons dark brown sugar
80 ml balsamic vinegar
20 g unsalted butter
3 large cloves garlic, finely chopped
4 portobello or other large flat mushrooms, thinly sliced
3 sprigs thyme, leaves stripped
8 flour tortillas or wholegrain wraps
200 g cheddar, grated
1 handful baby rocket leaves, roughly chopped
sour cream and lemon wedges, to serve

Serves 4

Heat half the oil in a heavy-based frying pan over low heat. Add the onion and cook, stirring, for 10–12 minutes or until soft. Add the sugar and balsamic vinegar and cook, stirring, for 7 minutes or until the onion is caramelised and the liquid has reduced. Transfer the onion mixture to a bowl and wipe the pan clean.

Heat the butter and remaining oil in the frying pan over medium heat. Add the garlic, mushroom and thyme and cook, stirring often, for 3–4 minutes or until the mushroom is soft. Remove the pan from the heat and set aside.

Heat a chargrill pan or a large non-stick frying pan over medium–high heat. Working one at a time, lightly toast the tortillas on one side for 1 minute, then set aside on a plate.

Place half the tortillas, toasted-side up, on a clean surface. Divide the caramelised onion mixture, mushroom mixture, grated cheese and rocket among the bases, then pop the remaining tortillas, toasted-side down, on top.

Return the pan to medium–high heat. Add a quesadilla and cook for 1–2 minutes until toasted, then carefully flip with a spatula and cook for 1 minute. Transfer to a plate and keep warm while you repeat with the remaining quesadillas.

Cut into quarters and serve warm with sour cream and lemon wedges alongside.

INSPIRED BY A MEAL ENJOYED IN NEW YORK

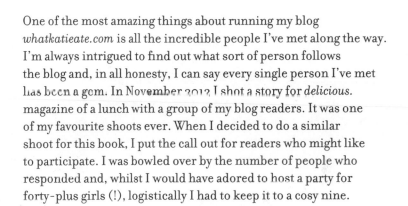

JESS

PETA

One of the most amazing things about running my blog *whatkatieate.com* is all the incredible people I've met along the way. I'm always intrigued to find out what sort of person follows the blog and, in all honesty, I can say every single person I've met has been a gem. In November 2012 I shot a story for *delicious.* magazine of a lunch with a group of my blog readers. It was one of my favourite shoots ever. When I decided to do a similar shoot for this book, I put the call out for readers who might like to participate. I was bowled over by the number of people who responded and, whilst I would have adored to host a party for forty-plus girls (!), logistically I had to keep it to a cosy nine.

Girls for lunch

The day went brilliantly. I arrived at the studio with my assistants Lou and Madeleine to find nine of the most sociable, gorgeous girls, totally chilled out, enthusiastically chatting with each other. They were all so incredibly lovely and warm. It was amazing to see how well they all got on — I think some lasting friendships were made that day. I was particularly touched to see Katische again — I had met her at a talk I gave at Christmas and she had flown in from Perth just to be there, which was pretty special. I hope very much I get to see all the girls again soon — but next time, I'll leave the frantic cooking, styling and shooting out of it, and we'll all just head to the pub for a drink.

Thank you again to Ange, Angela, Belinda, Dara, Jess, Katische, Louise, Peta (and her hubby, who was an AMAZING washer-upper and all-round super-help on the day) and Phillipa.

MENU

Pomegranate chicken page 97

Bulgar wheat and herbs with semi-dried tomatoes page 49

Indian-spiced lamb cutlets page 106

Double choc brownies with salted butterscotch and cherries page 283

Raspberry and pomegranate 'martinis' page 246

PIZZA, PASTA, BREAD

TOMATO, COURGETTE FLOWER AND SALAMI PIZZAS

A pretty, summery pizza bursting with fresh flavours. You can make the pizza dough in advance; wrapped tightly in cling film it will keep for up to 2 days in the fridge or 1 month in the freezer.

№. 193

8 slices provolone cheese
20 thin slices spicy salami
10 baby courgettes with flowers attached, courgettes
    thinly sliced, flowers halved lengthways and stamens
    removed
1 × 250 g punnet baby vine-ripened tomatoes
oregano, freshly ground black pepper and extra
    virgin olive oil, to serve

PIZZA DOUGH
400 g strong flour
fine salt
¾ teaspoon dried yeast
1½ tablespoons extra virgin olive oil

PIZZA SAUCE
olive oil, for cooking
1 small brown onion, finely chopped
3 cloves garlic, finely chopped
1 × 400 g tin chopped tomatoes
260 g tomato passata
pinch of chilli flakes
pinch of caster sugar
10 large basil leaves, torn
sea salt and freshly ground black pepper

Makes 2 × 32 cm pizzas (serves 4)

For the pizza dough, sift the flour into a large bowl. Make a well in the centre and add a pinch of salt along with the yeast, oil and 200 ml lukewarm water. Whisk with a fork, gradually incorporating the flour from the sides. Using clean hands, bring the mixture together to form a dough, then transfer to a floured surface. Knead the dough firmly for 5 minutes, really stretching it out as you go. (Alternatively, you can use a stand mixer fitted with a dough hook. Mix all the ingredients on medium speed until combined, then mix on low speed for 5 minutes.)

Place the dough in a bowl, cover with a damp tea towel and leave in a warm place to rise for 1 hour or until doubled in size.

Meanwhile, for the sauce, warm 1 tablespoon oil in a saucepan over low heat, then add the onion and garlic and cook, stirring often, for 3–4 minutes or until softened. Add the tomato, passata, chilli flakes, sugar and basil and simmer over low–medium heat, stirring often, for 15–18 minutes or until the sauce has thickened and reduced by about one-third. Season with salt and pepper and set aside.

Preheat the oven to 260°C/240°C fan/gas 10.

Turn the dough out onto a floured surface and cut in half. Place each piece on an oiled 32 cm pizza tray and, using your hands, gently stretch the dough to fit the trays. Divide the pizza sauce between the bases and spread evenly. Top with the cheese, salami, courgette, courgette flowers and tomatoes.

Bake for 12–15 minutes until golden brown around the edges. Serve scattered with oregano, a good grinding of pepper and a drizzle of extra virgin olive oil.

KATIE'S HAWAIIAN PIZZAS

I love pizza. I could eat it every day, especially if it has a really good, thin, crispy base. But I have to say – and I'm going to admit this in print, ironically in a publication that I'm hoping millions of people will read – that my favourite pizza topping is ham and pineapple. At dinner with friends, I get teased mercilessly about it, so I'm taking a stand for all you H&P pizza lovers out there, and I've created a 'fancy gourmet' version of this classic that we can all be proud of.

1 quantity Pizza Dough (see page 193)
250 g buffalo mozzarella, sliced
8 thin slices prosciutto
olive oil, for drizzling
freshly ground black pepper

BARBECUE SAUCE
2 tablespoons olive oil
1 small red onion, finely chopped
4 cloves garlic, finely chopped
3 teaspoons smoked paprika
1 tablespoon brown sugar
1 tablespoon Worcestershire sauce
500 ml tomato passata

PINEAPPLE SALSA
1 red onion, finely diced
3 cloves garlic, finely chopped
1 long green chilli, seeded and finely diced
300 g drained tinned pineapple slices, finely chopped
250 g tomatoes, finely diced
finely grated zest of 1 lime
70 g unsalted peanuts, finely chopped
1 small handful each coriander and mint, finely chopped
sea salt and freshly ground black pepper

Makes 2 × 32 cm pizzas (serves 4)

For the barbecue sauce, heat the oil in a large frying pan over medium heat. Add the onion and garlic and cook, stirring, for 2–3 minutes or until softened. Stir in the paprika and sugar and cook for 1 minute. Add the Worcestershire sauce and passata and cook, stirring, for 10–12 minutes or until reduced by about one-third. Remove from the heat and set aside.

For the pineapple salsa, combine all the ingredients in a bowl. Tip into a sieve and set aside to allow any excess moisture to drain off.

Preheat the oven to 260°C/240°C fan/gas 10.

Turn the dough out onto a floured surface and cut in half. Place each piece on an oiled 32 cm pizza tray and, using your hands, gently stretch the dough to fit the trays. Divide the barbecue sauce between the pizza bases and spread out evenly. Spoon one-third of the salsa onto each base, reserving the rest, then add the mozzarella and prosciutto and drizzle with oil.

Bake for 12–15 minutes until golden brown around the edges. Serve with plenty of freshly ground black pepper and the remaining pineapple salsa dolloped on top, if you like.

GREEN PIZZAS WITH MUSHROOMS

This is one of my sneaky healthy recipes – the green sauce is full of kale and walnuts, and you could substitute cottage cheese for the goat's cheese if you like. You'll have some sauce left over, which is perfect tossed through freshly cooked pasta the next day. You can use ordinary kale leaves with the central stems removed if you can't get hold of baby kale.

1 quantity Pizza Dough (see page 193)
50 g shiitake mushrooms, sliced
50 g Swiss brown mushrooms, sliced
150 g soft goat's cheese, sliced into rounds
sea salt and freshly ground black pepper
2 tablespoons extra virgin olive oil
toasted slivered almonds and baby kale leaves, to serve

GREEN SAUCE
50 g rocket leaves
50 g baby kale leaves
70 g broccoli florets
3 cloves garlic
70 g almonds
1 handful basil
50 g parmesan, grated
125 ml light olive oil
1 tablespoon lemon juice
sea salt and freshly ground black pepper

Makes 2 × 32 cm pizzas (serves 4)

For the sauce, place all the ingredients in a food processor and process until thick and combined.

Preheat the oven to 260°C/240°C fan/gas 10.

Turn the dough out onto a floured surface and cut in half. Place each piece on an oiled 32 cm pizza tray and, using your hands, gently stretch the dough to fit the trays.

Spread about one-third of the sauce onto each pizza base (the remaining green sauce will keep in an airtight container in the fridge for 1 day). Divide the mushrooms and goat's cheese between the bases, season generously and drizzle with oil.

Bake for 12–15 minutes until golden brown around the edges. Serve topped with toasted slivered almonds and baby kale.

SPAGHETTI WITH BACON, CAPERS AND MINT

This simple, yet elegant pasta dish was inspired by my travels in Italy. It uses just a few ingredients and is equally good as a weeknight meal or piled onto a platter as part of a spread to feed a crowd.

1 tablespoon olive oil, plus extra for drizzling
1 brown onion, finely diced
200 g free-range bacon, fat and rind removed, diced
2 cloves garlic, finely chopped
500 g cherry tomatoes, halved, juice and seeds squeezed out
sea salt
65 g salted capers, well rinsed
6 sprigs mint, leaves picked and torn
400 g spaghetti
finely grated parmesan, to serve

Serves 4

Heat the oil in a large non-stick frying pan over medium heat and cook the onion, stirring often, for 3–4 minutes or until starting to soften. Add the bacon and cook, stirring often, for 4–5 minutes or until lightly browned. Add the garlic and cook, stirring, for 30 seconds.

Add the squeezed tomato halves and a good pinch of salt, then reduce the heat to low–medium and simmer for 5–6 minutes. Add the capers and mint, stir to combine and simmer for 1–2 minutes.

Meanwhile, cook the spaghetti according to the packet instructions. Drain, reserving the cooking water, then immediately add to the frying pan and toss together with the other ingredients, adding a little cooking water to moisten. Serve hot with grated parmesan.

C.L.E. HAIGH
GRAINSBY.

Red
PePPerS
3 FOR £1

SPAGHETTI WITH ALMOND, MINT AND BASIL PESTO

This pesto is slightly sweeter than the traditional version due to the inclusion of mint. Any leftover pesto can be stored for up to 2 days in the fridge.

1 large bunch basil, leaves picked
1 bunch mint, leaves picked
2 cloves garlic, peeled
250 ml extra virgin olive oil
70 g blanched almonds
100 g parmesan, finely grated, plus extra to serve
400 g spaghetti
extra virgin olive oil, for drizzling

Serves 4

Place the basil and most of the mint in a food processor (set aside a few small mint leaves to use as a garnish). Add the garlic, olive oil, almonds, parmesan and 1 tablespoon water and whiz to a smooth, thick paste.

Cook the spaghetti according to the packet instructions, then drain, reserving the cooking water, and transfer to a large bowl.

Stir the pesto and a few tablespoons of the reserved cooking water through the pasta to coat. Serve immediately topped with extra parmesan, a drizzle of olive oil and a few small mint leaves.

CRAB, LEMON AND CHILLI SPAGHETTI

I buy crab meat in 150 g packs; you could buy a whole crab and pick the meat yourself, but it will be a lot messier! This is a light summery pasta dish for a weekend lunch. Serve with crusty bread and some chilled white wine.

160 ml olive oil
140 g fresh breadcrumbs
finely grated zest and juice of 1 lemon
sea salt and freshly ground black pepper
1 handful flat-leaf parsley, finely chopped
400 g spaghetti
1 onion, finely chopped
3 cloves garlic, finely chopped
1 long red chilli, seeded and finely chopped
300 g cooked crab meat, drained and shredded if chunky
lemon wedges, to serve

Serves 4

Heat 60 ml of the oil in a large frying pan over medium heat. Add the breadcrumbs, lemon zest and salt and pepper, then cook, stirring, for 6–8 minutes or until toasted and lightly golden. Transfer to a bowl to cool, then stir through the parsley and set aside.

Cook the spaghetti according to the packet instructions, then drain, reserving the cooking water.

Meanwhile, wipe the frying pan clean, add 1 tablespoon of the oil and place over medium heat. Cook the onion and garlic, stirring, for 4–5 minutes or until softened. Add the chilli and cook for 1 minute, then add the crab and cook, stirring, for 1 minute or until warmed through.

Add the lemon juice and the remaining oil to the pan and stir to combine. Simmer over low heat, stirring occasionally, for 2 minutes to allow the flavours to infuse.

Add the hot drained pasta to the pan along with a few tablespoons of the cooking water to moisten. Toss together to combine well, then add half the breadcrumb mixture and toss again to combine.

Transfer to a platter and scatter over the remaining breadcrumb mixture. Serve immediately with lemon wedges to the side.

AUBERGINE AND MOZZARELLA LASAGNE

This is a perfect vegetarian main course. It takes about 1½ hours to salt and grill the aubergine, but you can do this the day before if you like. I use a 32 cm ×x 20 cm ×x 6 cm baking dish for this.

2 aubergines, sliced lengthways into 5 mm thick slices
fine salt
1½ tablespoons olive oil
1 brown onion, coarsely chopped
4 cloves garlic, coarsely chopped
1 long red chilli, seeded and finely chopped
2 × 400 g tins chopped tomatoes
1 tablespoon tomato puree
250 ml good-quality red wine
1 tablespoon balsamic vinegar
1 tablespoon salted capers, well rinsed
1 bunch oregano, leaves stripped and roughly torn

pinch of caster sugar
freshly ground black pepper
olive oil spray
40 g fresh white bread or sourdough
150 g finely grated parmesan
2 courgettes, coarsely grated
2 tablespoons light sour cream
250 g buffalo mozzarella, thinly sliced
100 g fresh pasta sheets, cut to size

Serves 6

Place the aubergine slices in a large colander and sprinkle with 2 tablespoons salt. Toss to coat, then leave to stand for 1 hour.

Meanwhile, heat 1 tablespoon oil in a large heavy-based saucepan over medium heat. Add the onion and cook for 3–4 minutes until softened, then add the garlic and cook for 3 minutes, stirring often so the garlic doesn't burn. Add the chilli and cook for 2 minutes, stirring often. Add the tinned tomatoes, tomato puree, red wine, balsamic vinegar, capers, most of the oregano (saving a large handful for the crumb mixture) and the sugar and season with pepper. Stir to combine, then simmer over low heat for 45 minutes.

Thoroughly rinse the aubergine slices under cold running water, then lay them out on kitchen roll, patting with extra kitchen roll to dry thoroughly. Spray olive oil on one side of each slice, then place under the oven grill, oil-side up, and grill for 3–4 minutes. Remove from the grill, turn the slices over and spray with olive oil, then grill until golden brown. Drain on kitchen roll.

Preheat the oven to 200°C/180°C fan/gas 6.

Whiz the bread in a food processor to make coarse crumbs. Add the reserved oregano and whiz to combine, then add 50 g of the parmesan and pulse to combine. Set aside.

Squeeze the excess water from the grated courgette and pat dry with kitchen roll. Heat the remaining oil in a frying pan over medium heat, add the courgette and cook for 3 minutes, stirring often. Reduce the heat to low, add the sour cream and cook, stirring, for 1–2 minutes.

To assemble, spoon half the tomato sauce into the base of a large rectangular baking dish. Top with around half the aubergine slices, arranging them in a layer and slightly overlapping them. Add half the sliced mozzarella, half the remaining parmesan and then a layer of pasta sheets.

Add another layer of tomato sauce, aubergine, mozzarella, parmesan and pasta sheets, then top the pasta layer with the courgette mixture, any remaining aubergine slices and the herbed breadcrumbs.

Bake for 35–40 minutes or until golden brown and bubbling, then slice and serve.

WALNUT BREAD

This is quick to make, nutty and textural and always tastes great. I like to serve
it with the carrot and ginger soup on page 70.

2 teaspoons brown sugar
1 × 7 g sachet instant dried yeast
3 tablespoons olive oil
300 g plain flour, sifted
150 g buckwheat flour, sifted
2 tablespoons wheatgerm
175 g walnuts, toasted and finely chopped
1½ tablespoons chia seeds
sea salt and freshly ground black pepper
20 g unsalted butter, melted

Makes 2 small loaves

Combine the sugar, yeast and 125 ml warm water in a large bowl.
Cover and leave to stand for 10–12 minutes until frothy. Stir in the oil and
another 160 ml lukewarm water, then add the flours, wheatgerm, walnuts,
1 tablespoon of the chia seeds and 1 teaspoon salt. Stir to combine, then use
your hands to form the mixture into a dough.

Turn out onto a floured surface and knead for 5 minutes or until smooth.
Place in a clean bowl, cover with cling film and set aside in a warm place
for 2 hours or until doubled in size.

Preheat the oven to 220°C/200°C fan/gas 7 and sprinkle flour over a large
baking tray.

Turn the dough out onto a clean floured surface and knead once or twice to knock
out the air. Divide in half and shape into two loaves. Place on the prepared tray,
then cut three evenly spaced, 1 cm-deep slashes on an angle across each loaf.
Brush the tops with melted butter and scatter over the remaining chia seeds.

Bake for 20–25 minutes or until golden and the bases sound hollow when tapped.

SEEDED BAGELS WITH SMOKED SALMON

I always thought bagels would be difficult to make, but they are surprisingly easy. These are great for a cocktail party, or to serve as little hunger busters late at night after a few drinks. Fill them with anything you please: cured meats, pickles and mayo, or roast beef, watercress and horseradish sauce would be delicious, too.

No. 211

1 tablespoon olive oil or rice bran oil
1 brown onion, finely chopped
2 large cloves garlic, finely chopped
1 tablespoon chia seeds
1 tablespoon white sesame seeds
1 tablespoon black sesame seeds
1 tablespoon poppy seeds
60 g pine nuts
1 × 7 g sachet instant dried yeast
1 tablespoon caster sugar
450 g strong flour (at least 13% gluten)

1 teaspoon fine salt
4 tablespoons light agave nectar (see page 10)
250 g light cream cheese
2 tablespoons creme fraiche
1 tablespoon lemon juice
1 small handful dill, snipped
400 g smoked salmon slices
sea salt and freshly ground black pepper
lemon wedges, to serve

Makes 16

Heat the oil in a small frying pan over medium heat, and cook the onion for 3 minutes or until just softened. Add the garlic and cook for 3 minutes, stirring often, until the onion is cooked through and translucent. Remove from the heat and leave to cool for 10 minutes.

Combine the seeds and pine nuts in a bowl and set aside.

Combine the yeast, sugar and 100 ml warm water in a large bowl. Cover and leave to stand for 10–12 minutes until frothy. Stir in the flour, salt, cooled onion and garlic, half the seed mixture and 200 ml warm water. Mix everything together well with your hands and turn out onto a well-floured surface.

Knead the dough for 10 minutes, stretching it out as you go, then shape into a ball. Place in a large bowl that has been greased with olive oil and cover with a damp tea towel. Set aside in a warm place for 1 hour or until doubled in size.

Preheat the oven to 190°C/170°C fan/gas 5 and line two baking trays with greaseproof paper.

Half-fill a large saucepan with water and bring to a boil.

Stir in the agave nectar.

Punch down the dough with your fist and turn out onto a floured surface. Divide the dough into sixteen equal portions (each the size of a small egg) and form into balls. Slightly flatten each one, then use a 2 cm plain round cutter to cut a hole out of the centres. Swirl each bagel gently on your floured index finger until slightly stretched.

Working in batches of four at a time, place the bagels in the boiling water and cook for 1 minute, then flip with a slotted spoon and cook on the other side for 1 minute. Scoop out and leave to drain on kitchen roll.

Arrange the boiled bagels on the prepared trays and evenly scatter the remaining seed mixture over the top. Bake for 30 minutes or until golden brown and glossy.

Meanwhile, whisk together the cream cheese, creme fraiche, lemon juice and dill in a bowl and refrigerate for 20 minutes.

Halve the bagels horizontally and smear the bases with the chilled cream-cheese mixture. Top with smoked salmon, season well and pop on the lids. Serve with lemon wedges.

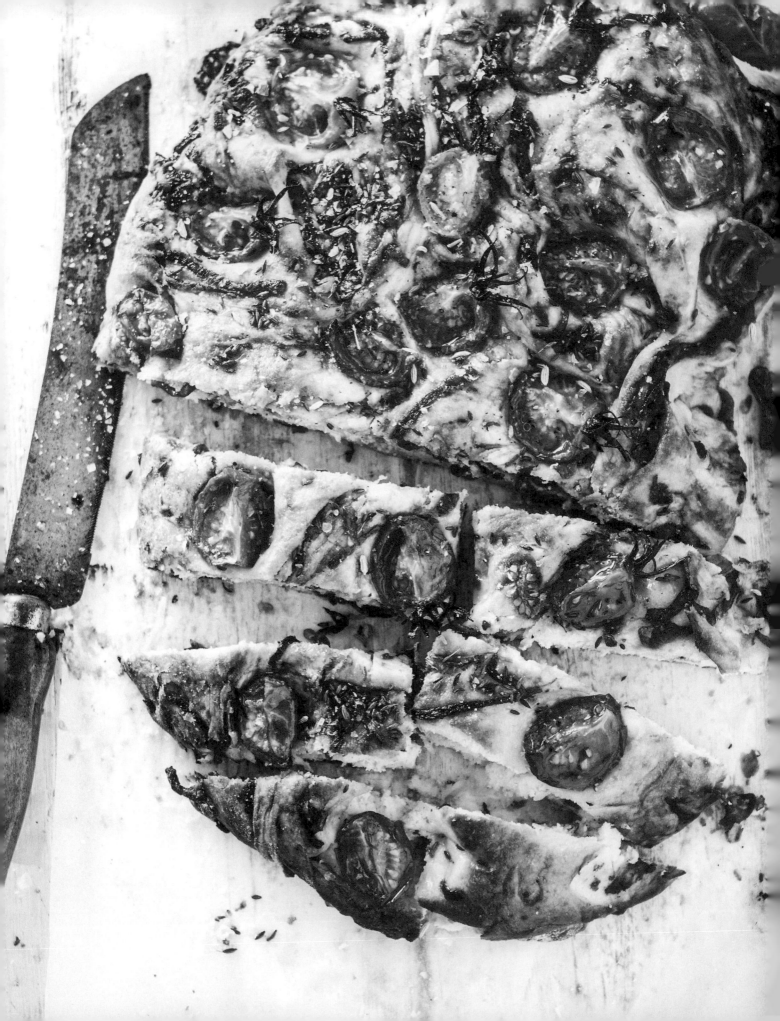

CARAMELISED ONION, FENNEL AND TOMATO FOCACCIA

This is a really flavoursome bread: give it a generous seasoning of sea salt before cooking to bring out the flavours. Serve it with a good-quality extra virgin olive oil to dip into.

1 × 7 g sachet instant dried yeast
2 pinches of caster sugar
80 ml olive oil, plus extra for brushing
450 g strong flour
fine salt
4 red onions, finely sliced
1½ tablespoons brown sugar
4 tablespoons balsamic vinegar
2 teaspoons fennel seeds
1 × 250 g punnet cherry tomatoes, halved
sea salt

Serves 8

Combine the yeast, sugar, 2 tablespoons oil and 320 ml warm water in a bowl, then set aside in a warm place for 5 minutes or until frothy.

Sift the flour into a bowl and add 1 teaspoon salt. Make a well in the centre, pour in the yeast mixture and stir to combine.

Turn out onto a lightly floured surface and knead for 10 minutes or until smooth and elastic. Place in a large bowl that has been greased with a little olive oil and cover with a damp tea towel. Set aside in a warm place for 1 hour or until doubled in size.

Meanwhile, heat the remaining oil in a frying pan over low–medium heat. Add the onion and cook, stirring, for 12–15 minutes or until soft. Add the brown sugar and vinegar and cook, stirring, for 7–10 minutes or until the onion is caramelised and the vinegar has been absorbed. Remove the pan from the heat and set aside.

Punch down the dough with your fist. Turn out onto a lightly floured surface and knead for 1–2 minutes.

Spread the dough out to form a rough rectangle, then cover the surface evenly with the onion mixture. Scatter the fennel seeds on top, reserving a few to scatter over the cooked focaccia. Carefully fold the dough over on itself a few times until most of the onion mixture is incorporated into the dough (this bit can get a little sticky so ensure your work surface is well-floured).

Preheat the oven to 220°C/200°C fan/gas 7 and grease a baking tray with olive oil.

Press the dough into the prepared tray, cover with a damp tea towel and set aside in a warm, draught-free place for 20 minutes or until doubled in volume.

Use your finger to press dimples into the dough, then carefully press the tomato halves into the dimples. Brush well with oil and sprinkle over the remaining fennel seeds, then season with a few good pinches of sea salt.

Bake for 20–25 minutes or until golden and cooked through. Serve warm or at room temperature.

PARTY FOOD AND DRINKS

SPICED ALMONDS

My friend Michael Wohlstadt from Dairyman's Cottage in the
Barossa Valley (see pages 32–41) greets visitors to his guesthouse
with the most incredible tray of breakfast goodies plus a beautiful
bottle of wine and these amazing spiced nuts. I gobbled up so
many of them during my stay there that I knew I had to include
this recipe in the book.

300 g almonds
60 ml olive oil
1 tablespoon sea salt
2 tablespoons very finely chopped kaffir lime leaves
1½ tablespoons dried garlic granules
3 teaspoons dried chilli flakes
1½ teaspoons sweet paprika
1 teaspoon chilli powder

Serves 1–2

Preheat the oven to 240°C/220°C fan/gas 9.

Place the almonds on a baking tray, drizzle with oil and season
with salt. Spread the almonds out over the tray, then roast for
10 minutes, tossing now and then, or until some of the nuts split.

Remove the tray from the oven and sprinkle over the lime leaves
and spices while the almonds are hot. Toss to combine,
then leave to cool on the tray.

Store in an airtight container for up to 1 week.

EDAMAME BEANS WITH MIRIN, SALT AND CHILLI

These are really quick to prepare and incredibly tasty — you'll be addicted in seconds. Brilliant for a cocktail party or pre-dinner nibbles.

450 g frozen edamame beans
1 tablespoon sesame oil
1 tablespoon mirin
1 tablespoon rice wine vinegar
2 teaspoons dried chilli flakes, plus extra for serving
sea salt

Serves 4–8

Place the edamame beans in a heatproof bowl, cover with cling film and microwave on high for 4 minutes.

Meanwhile, whisk together the sesame oil, mirin and rice wine vinegar in a bowl.

Pour the dressing over the beans, then season with chilli flakes and 2 teaspoons salt and mix to coat well.

Serve on a large plate, with extra salt and chilli flakes to the side.

WASABI STRAWS WITH SALMON DIPPING SAUCE

Perfect for parties, these straws have a bit of a kick which is contrasted perfectly by the smooth and creamy dip. You can make the straws as long or short as you like.

250 g plain flour
1 teaspoon instant dried yeast
2 teaspoons black sesame seeds, plus extra for baking
3 teaspoons wasabi paste
sea salt and freshly ground black pepper

SALMON DIPPING SAUCE
240 g light sour cream
1 tablespoon tamari or soy sauce
juice of ½ lemon
250 g smoked salmon, torn
sea salt and freshly ground black pepper

Makes 40

Place the flour, yeast, sesame seeds, wasabi and ½ teaspoon salt in a stand mixer fitted with a dough hook. Add 160 ml warm water and mix on low speed for 5 minutes or until smooth.

Turn out onto a lightly floured surface and knead for a couple of minutes, then shape into a ball and place in a large bowl that has been greased with a little olive oil. Cover with a damp tea towel and leave to rest in a warm place for 1 hour or until the dough has doubled in size.

Preheat the oven to 190°C/170°C fan/gas 5 and line three baking trays with greaseproof paper.

Pick off walnut-sized balls of dough and, on a clean surface, roll them out to 20 cm long sticks. Place on the baking trays, brush with a little water and scatter over the extra sesame seeds. Bake for 15–20 minutes or until golden brown and crisp.

Meanwhile, for the dipping sauce, place all the ingredients in a food processor and whiz until the smoked salmon is incorporated and the sauce is smooth. Season to taste and set aside.

Serve the straws stacked on a platter with the dipping sauce alongside.

KATIE'S PÂTÉ WITH RHUBARB PASTE AND GLAZED PEARS

I'm a huge pâté fan and could eat it until it came out of my ears. For this one you'll probably need to order the duck livers in advance from your butcher. I use amontillado or oloroso sherry, but whatever you can get your hands on will be fine.

150 g butter
3 golden shallots, finely sliced
4 large cloves garlic, finely sliced
250 g free-range bacon, fat and rind removed, diced
60 ml semi-sweet sherry
250 g free-range chicken livers, trimmed
250 g free-range duck livers, trimmed
2–3 sprigs thyme, leaves stripped
300 ml whipping cream
sea salt and freshly ground white pepper
sourdough bread, thinly sliced and toasted, to serve

RHUBARB PASTE

¾ bunch rhubarb, trimmed and cut into 1.5 cm pieces (you'll need 240 g trimmed rhubarb)
2 tablespoons caster sugar
125 ml blood orange juice or orange juice
2 teaspoons Grand Marnier
3 sheets gelatine

GLAZED PEARS

4 pears, peeled, cored and cut into eight wedges
4 star anise
5 cardamom pods, bruised with the back of a knife
2 tablespoons dark brown sugar

Serves 10–12

Melt half the butter in a frying pan over medium heat. Add the shallot and garlic and cook, stirring, for 3–4 minutes or until softened. Add the bacon and cook, stirring often, for 6–8 minutes or until just golden brown. Add a tablespoon of the sherry and stir with a wooden spoon, scraping up any bits stuck to the bottom of the pan. Transfer the mixture to a blender.

In the same pan, melt the remaining butter over medium heat, then add the chicken and duck livers and the thyme and cook for 3–4 minutes or until the livers are just cooked but still a little pink in the middle. Add the cream and remaining sherry and stir to coat, then transfer to the blender. Blend all the ingredients until smooth. Season with salt and pepper and leave to cool for 15 minutes before transferring to sterilised jars. Set aside.

For the rhubarb paste, place the rhubarb, sugar, orange juice, Grand Marnier and 100 ml water in a saucepan and bring to a boil. Reduce the heat to low–medium and simmer for 8–10 minutes, or until the rhubarb has collapsed and the sauce is thick. Strain through a fine-meshed sieve into a bowl and set aside to cool.

Place the gelatine sheets in a bowl and cover with cold water. Leave to stand for 5 minutes, then remove and squeeze out the excess water. Place them in a small saucepan with 2 tablespoons of the strained rhubarb sauce and stir over medium heat until smooth. Transfer the gelatine mixture to the bowl with the remaining rhubarb sauce and combine well. Spoon evenly over the pâté in the jars, seal and refrigerate overnight.

For the glazed pears, place all the ingredients and 750 ml water in a saucepan over high heat. Bring to a boil, then reduce the heat to low and cook for 5–10 minutes, or until the pears are tender when pierced with a knife (the cooking time will depend on the ripeness of the pears). Remove the pears with a slotted spoon and set aside in a bowl, then simmer the poaching liquid over medium–high heat for 25–30 minutes or until reduced to a glaze. Return the pears to the sauce and simmer for 3–4 minutes, stirring gently, until the pears are glazed. Set aside to cool.

Serve the pâté with the glazed pears and plenty of toasted sourdough.

PRAWN CROSTINI WITH TOMATO AND CHAMPAGNE SAUCE

No. 229

If you really want to splurge, you can opt to use lobster tail meat in this dish instead of the prawns. Try to get the best hollandaise sauce you can, as it makes all the difference.

toasted baguette slices and bought hollandaise sauce, to serve
600 g cooked prawns, peeled and deveined
dill sprigs and freshly ground black pepper, to garnish

TOMATO AND CHAMPAGNE SAUCE
3 large vine-ripened tomatoes
pinch of caster sugar
50 g unsalted butter, plus extra for cooking
250 ml champagne or sparkling wine
Tabasco sauce, to taste
sea salt and freshly ground white pepper

Makes 12

For the sauce, cut the tomatoes in half and squeeze the seeds and juice into a small saucepan over low heat. Finely chop the flesh and add to the pan. Increase the heat to medium and cook for 2–3 minutes. Add the sugar and butter and cook until the butter has melted, then add the champagne or sparkling wine and simmer for 10 minutes or until the sauce has thickened and reduced slightly.

Transfer to a blender and whiz until smooth, then push through a fine-meshed sieve back into the pan. Place over low heat and simmer for 40–50 minutes, stirring occasionally, until thickened. Add an extra small knob of butter, a dash or two of Tabasco and season, then remove from the heat.

Spread each slice of toast with a teaspoon of hollandaise sauce and top with one or two prawns. Drizzle with a teaspoon of the sauce and garnish with dill sprigs. Season with a little pepper and serve.

FETA CROSTINI WITH COURGETTE AND PROSCIUTTO

Use a baguette or other light bread for these – not a sourdough as it will be too heavy. I use a mandoline to thinly slice the courgette: it's a great tool in the kitchen. Remember to cut the prosciutto into bite-sized pieces so they're not too messy to eat.

1 large courgette, very finely sliced with a mandoline
finely grated zest and juice of 1 lemon, plus extra juice for cooking, and zest to serve
2 tablespoons olive oil
sea salt and freshly ground black pepper
60 g frozen baby peas
½ crusty baguette, cut into 12 × 1.5 cm thick slices on the diagonal
1 clove garlic, halved
250 g marinated feta, drained
1 handful mint, finely chopped, plus extra leaves to serve
6 thin slices prosciutto, cut into bite-sized pieces
extra virgin olive oil, to serve

Makes 12

Combine the courgette, lemon juice and 1 tablespoon oil in a bowl. Season and set aside for 15 minutes.

Meanwhile, blanch the peas in boiling water with a squeeze of lemon juice added for 30 seconds, then drain and set aside.

Heat a chargrill pan over medium–high heat. Brush the bread on both sides with the remaining oil, then grill for 1–2 minutes on each side until golden and charred. Rub the bread on one side with the cut-side of the garlic, then set aside.

Drain the courgette, reserving the marinade, and place on the hot grill for 1 minute each side or until tender and lightly charred.

Add the feta, lemon zest and mint to the reserved marinade, season well and combine to a smooth paste. Spread the paste onto the bread slices, and top with prosciutto, courgette and peas. Garnish with extra lemon zest and mint leaves, then drizzle with a little extra virgin olive oil, season and serve.

O'SHOCKO'S GUACO WITH CRISPY LIME TORTILLA CHIPS

My good friend Ian O'Shaughnessy makes the best-ever guacamole on the planet. Use just-ripe avocados and take care not to over-mash them, or the end result will look like baby food. *Arriba!*

finely grated zest of 2 limes, plus extra lime wedges, to serve
sea salt and freshly ground black pepper
8 soft corn or flour tortillas, each cut into eight wedges
2 cloves garlic, halved
light olive oil spray

O'SHOCKO'S GUACO
3 vine-ripened tomatoes
boiling water, for blanching
flesh of 3 avocados
finely grated zest of 1 lime
juice of 2 limes
½ small red onion, very finely chopped
3 cloves garlic, very finely chopped
1 small handful coriander, very finely chopped
2 teaspoons chipotle sauce (see page 28) or a few dashes of Tabasco sauce
sea salt and freshly ground black pepper

Serves 6

For the guacamole, cut a small cross in the base of each tomato, then place them in a heatproof bowl and cover with boiling water. Leave for 30 seconds, then plunge the tomatoes into cold water to refresh before carefully peeling. Cut the peeled tomatoes in half, scoop out the seeds and discard, then finely chop the flesh.

Place the avocado flesh, lime zest and juice in a mixing bowl. Gently mash to a coarse texture using a fork. Add the tomato, onion, finely chopped garlic, coriander and chipotle or Tabasco sauce. Gently fold together to combine, taking care not to break up the avocado too much, then season to taste. Cover and place in the fridge to chill.

Preheat the oven to 200°C/180°C fan/gas 6 and line three large baking trays with greaseproof paper.

Place the lime zest in a small jar with a lid, add a good pinch of salt and some pepper, then close the lid and shake to combine.

Arrange the tortilla wedges on the prepared trays and rub the tops with the cut-side of the garlic. Spray with olive oil, then scatter over the spiced zest. Bake for 10–12 minutes or until golden brown and crisp, then leave to cool.

Serve the chips with the chilled guaco and extra lime wedges to the side.

PORK AND PICKLED ONION PASTIES

These are perfect for a weekend picnic or to pack into school lunch boxes.
I use good old, English-style brown pickled onions, an all-rounder potato like
desiree, and a crumbly, sharp vintage cheddar for this recipe. You can use bought
shortcrust pastry if you are short of time.

125 g potatoes, diced
1 tablespoon olive oil
½ small brown onion, finely chopped
2 cloves garlic, finely chopped
200 g lean minced free-range pork
5 pickled onions, drained and chopped
75 g cheddar, chopped
1 tablespoon finely chopped flat-leaf parsley
sea salt and freshly ground black pepper
1 free-range egg yolk mixed with a little milk
1 tablespoon sesame seeds
good-quality tomato chutney, to serve

SOUR-CREAM PASTRY
200 g plain flour, sifted
150 g unsalted butter, chilled and cubed
60 g sour cream
freshly ground black pepper

Makes 8

For the pastry, place the flour and butter in the bowl of
a food processor and whiz until it resembles breadcrumbs.
Add the sour cream and black pepper and whiz until the
dough just starts to come together; it should be soft and
a little sticky to the touch.

Turn the dough out onto a lightly floured surface and
knead gently, shaping into a disc. Wrap in cling film
and refrigerate for 30 minutes.

Meanwhile, cook the potato in a saucepan of simmering
water for 12–15 minutes or until almost cooked but still
a little firm, then drain and set aside to cool.

Heat the oil in a large saucepan over medium heat. Add the
onion and cook, stirring, for 3–4 minutes or until softened.
Add the garlic and cook, stirring, for 2–3 minutes. Transfer
the mixture to a large bowl and set aside to cool, then add the
pork, pickled onion, cheese and parsley to the bowl, season
and mix together well. Add the potato and carefully fold it
through the mixture.

Preheat the oven to 200°C/180°C fan/gas 6 and line two
baking trays with greaseproof paper.

On a floured surface, divide the pastry into eight equal
portions and roll each portion out to a 14 cm round. Divide
the filling among the rounds, leaving a 1–2 cm border. Brush
the edges with eggwash, then fold one side over the other to
enclose the filling and form a semi-circle. Pinch the edges
together to seal, then stand the pastie so the join is at the top
and gently push the filling down to form a flat base.

Transfer the pasties to the prepared trays, brush the
tops with eggwash and scatter with sesame seeds.
Bake for 30 minutes or until the pastry is golden brown
and the filling is cooked through.

Serve hot or lukewarm with tomato chutney.

MEATBALL SLIDERS WITH TOMATO CHILLI SAUCE

Everyone loves sliders nowadays, and who can blame them? The following three recipes were inspired by a platter of sliders I've enjoyed on more than one occasion at a bar in the West Village in New York. If you can't get hold of fresh crabs for the crab sliders on page 239, use the tubs of crabmeat you can buy in some delis and supermarkets (just make sure you shred it well before use). I use a mandoline fitted with a 0.75 mm blade to finely shred the cabbage.

olive oil, for cooking
100 g fontina cheese, thinly sliced
1 large handful wild rocket leaves
20 seeded slider or baby brioche buns, halved horizontally

TOMATO CHILLI SAUCE

1 tablespoon olive oil
1 brown onion, finely chopped
3 cloves garlic, finely chopped
1 × 400 g tin chopped tomatoes
260 g tomato passata
pinch of dried chilli flakes
pinch of caster sugar
10 basil leaves, torn
sea salt and freshly ground black pepper

MEATBALLS

140 g sourdough bread, crusts removed
150 ml milk
400 g lean minced free-range beef
400 g lean minced free-range pork
½ brown onion, finely chopped
4 cloves garlic, finely chopped
2 tablespoons flat-leaf parsley, finely chopped
50 g parmesan, finely grated
pinch of grated nutmeg
1 tablespoon Worcestershire sauce
2 teaspoons wholegrain mustard
1 free-range egg
sea salt and freshly ground black pepper

Makes 20

For the sauce, heat the oil in a saucepan over medium–high heat, then add the onion and garlic and cook, stirring often, for 3–4 minutes. Add the tinned tomatoes, passata, chilli flakes, sugar and basil and simmer over low–medium heat, stirring often, for 15–18 minutes or until the sauce has reduced by about one-third. Season to taste with salt and pepper.

Meanwhile, for the meatballs, use your hands to combine all the ingredients in a large bowl.

Divide the mince mixture into twenty balls. Flatten them slightly and transfer to a kitchen roll-lined plate. Cover and refrigerate for 20 minutes.

Preheat the oven to 200°C/180°C fan/gas 6 and line two baking trays with greaseproof paper.

Heat 1 tablespoon oil in a large non-stick frying pan over medium heat. Working in batches of five at a time, cook the meatballs for 2–3 minutes on each side until golden brown, then transfer to the prepared trays. When they are all browned, place the trays in the oven and cook for 6–8 minutes. Remove and top each meatball with a slice of cheese, then return to the oven for 4–5 minutes until the cheese is melted and the meatballs are cooked to your liking. Set aside to rest for 10 minutes.

To assemble, place the rocket leaves on the bun bases and top with a meatball. Add 1 tablespoon tomato chilli sauce, then top with the bun lids and secure with a skewer.

MADE IN THE USA

L–R: MEATBALL SLIDERS WITH TOMATO CHILLI SAUCE; LOBSTER
SLIDERS WITH PEA MAYO; CRAB SLIDERS WITH CHIPOTLE MAYO SLAW

LOBSTER SLIDERS WITH PEA MAYO

(PICTURED PAGE 237)

16 thin slices mild pancetta
1 bunch rocket or watercress, leaves picked
16 seeded slider or baby brioche buns, halved horizontally
8 baby vine-ripened tomatoes, sliced
300 g lobster tail meat, flaked into bite-sized pieces

PEA MAYO
pinch of caster sugar
120 g frozen peas
2 free-range egg yolks
1 tablespoon lemon juice
sea salt and freshly ground white pepper
65 ml light olive oil
65 ml rapeseed oil
1 teaspoon Dijon mustard
2 teaspoons tarragon vinegar

Makes 16

Preheat the oven to 200°C/180°C fan/gas 6 and line a baking tray with greaseproof paper.

Spread the pancetta out onto the prepared tray and bake for 6–10 minutes or until crisp and browned, keeping an eye on it as it cooks.

Meanwhile, for the pea mayo, half-fill a small saucepan with cold water, add the caster sugar and bring to a boil. Add the peas and boil for 2 minutes, then drain and set aside to cool.

Place the egg yolks, lemon juice and a pinch of salt in the bowl of a food processor. Process on high speed for 1 minute then, with the motor running, add the oil in a thin, steady stream until the mixture is thick and glossy. Add the cooled peas, mustard and vinegar and season to taste with salt and pepper. Process again for 1 minute until the peas are finely minced and the mayo is a creamy pale-green colour.

To assemble, place some rocket or watercress on the bun bases and top with sliced tomato and pancetta. Add some lobster meat, then drizzle with pea mayo. Top with the bun lids and secure with a skewer.

CRAB SLIDERS WITH CHIPOTLE MAYO SLAW

(PICTURED PAGE 237)

4 tablespoons olive oil or rice bran oil

150 g red cabbage, finely shredded

1 large green apple, halved, cored and cut into thin
   matchsticks, then covered in a squeeze of lemon juice

50 g mangetout, finely sliced lengthways

20 seeded slider or baby brioche buns, halved
   horizontally

CRAB CAKES

140 g fresh white breadcrumbs

600 g cooked crab meat, drained
   and shredded if chunky

finely grated zest and juice of 1 lemon

2 tablespoons salted capers, well rinsed

140 g gherkins, drained well, very finely chopped

4 spring onions, trimmed and finely sliced

1 handful flat-leaf parsley, finely chopped

1 handful coriander, finely chopped

2 large free-range eggs, lightly whisked

sea salt and freshly ground black pepper

CHIPOTLE MAYO

2 free-range egg yolks

1 tablespoon lemon juice

sea salt and freshly ground white pepper

125 ml light olive oil

1 teaspoon wholegrain mustard

1 tablespoon apple cider vinegar

½ teaspoon sweet paprika

1 tablespoon chipotle sauce (see page 28)

Makes 20

For the crab cakes, use your hands to combine all the ingredients in a large bowl. Divide the mixture into twenty balls. Flatten them slightly and transfer to a paper-towel lined plate. Cover and refrigerate for 20 minutes.

For the chipotle mayo, place the egg yolks, lemon juice and a pinch of salt in the bowl of a food processor. Process on high speed for 1 minute then, with the motor running, add the oil in a thin, steady stream until the mixture is thick and glossy. Add the mustard, vinegar, paprika and chipotle sauce and season to taste with pepper, then process for 20 seconds. Set aside.

Preheat the oven to 200°C/180°C fan/gas 6 and line two baking trays with greaseproof paper.

Heat 1 tablespoon oil in a large non-stick frying pan over medium heat. Working in batches of five at a time, cook the crab cakes for 1–2 minutes on each side until lightly golden brown (handle them carefully as they are quite delicate), then transfer to the prepared trays. When they are all browned, place the trays in the oven and cook for 8–10 minutes or until golden brown and cooked through. Remove from the oven and keep warm.

Combine the cabbage, apple and mangetout in a bowl, then add the chipotle mayo and toss to coat well.

To assemble, place the crab cakes on the bun bases, then top with the slaw and the bun lids and secure with a skewer.

PRETZELS WITH CHOCOLATE AND SEA SALT

Yet another recipe inspired by a dinner in NYC, these are fab for parties:
the sea salt is a fantastic contrast to the bitter dark chocolate. Make them
as big or small as you like. Be sure to leave the pretzels in the boiling water
for only 30 seconds or they can become a little tough once baked. Serve
with small paper napkins to avoid messy chocolate fingers.

1¼ teaspoons brown sugar
1½ teaspoons dried yeast
350 g strong flour
1 tablespoon cocoa powder
fine salt
80 g bicarbonate of soda
400 g good-quality dark chocolate
1½ teaspoons sea salt

Makes 30

Sift the sugar, yeast, flour and cocoa into a bowl with
a good pinch of salt, then add 200 ml warm water. Stir
to combine then, using clean hands, form into a dough.
Turn out onto a lightly floured surface and knead for
4–5 minutes until smooth and elastic.

Place the dough in a large bowl greased with a little olive
oil and cover with a damp tea towel. Set aside in a warm
place for 1–2 hours or until doubled in size.

Turn the dough out onto a lightly floured surface and
shape into a log approximately 30 cm long. Using a
sharp knife, cut into 1 cm thick pieces, then roll out
each piece between your fingers to form a rope about
35–40 cm long. To form a pretzel shape, twist the ends
of the rope loosely together once or twice, leaving the
ends apart. Take either end of the rope and draw up and
over, then press into the middle of the looped section.
Moisten the join with a light brush of water and press
gently to seal. Place the pretzels on lightly greased
baking trays (spacing them out well) and set aside
for 20 minutes to rise.

Meanwhile, preheat the oven to 180°C/160°C fan/gas 4
and line two or three baking trays with greaseproof paper.

Place 4 litres water in a large saucepan over medium–
high heat, add the bicarbonate of soda and bring to
a low boil. Working one at a time, place each pretzel
in the water for 30 seconds, then remove with tongs
and drain on kitchen roll.

Arrange the pretzels on the prepared trays and bake
for 35–40 minutes.

Melt the chocolate in a heatproof bowl that fits snugly
over a saucepan of simmering water, then set aside to
cool slightly.

Leave the pretzels to cool completely before dipping
them in the melted chocolate to coat. Sprinkle with
sea salt, then refrigerate until the chocolate sets.

ORANGE AND CORIANDER MARGARITAS

(PICTURED PAGE 244)

These are fantastically refreshing on a warm day. If blood oranges aren't in season, any fresh orange will be wonderful. I use fine French Celtic salt to rim the glasses, but you can use any type of fine salt.

½ teaspoon coriander seeds
juice of 4 limes
juice of 8 blood oranges
120 ml tequila
60 ml Cointreau
2 teaspoons light agave nectar (see page 10)
crushed ice and bitters, to serve

Makes 4

Place the coriander seeds in a small frying pan over low heat.
Cook for 30–40 seconds or until fragrant, then crush using
a mortar and pestle.

Place the lime and orange juices, tequila, Cointreau and agave nectar
in a blender and blitz for a few seconds to combine. Add the crushed
coriander, then transfer to the fridge to chill for 30 minutes.

Strain the cocktail mixture into a jug. Fill four glasses with crushed ice,
then pour over the cocktail and add a dash of bitters to each.

PARTY FOOD AND DRINKS

This recipe was given to me by my mate, Andy Lawrence.
We met through work – he's a digital operator and fantastic
photographer – and he's assisted me with some of the shots
for this book. He's a great guy to work with.

During a cocktail party at my place, Andy, who's worked in bars
in the past, came up with this cracker. It's a take on a Bloody Mary,
minus the vodka. Feel free to add tequila to the mix, too, if you like
something a little stronger.

fine salt
1 lime, quartered
ice cubes
180 ml tomato juice
Worcestershire sauce
Tabasco sauce
sea salt and freshly ground black pepper
1 x 375 ml bottle Corona

Makes 1

Sprinkle some salt on a plate and spread out evenly. Rub a lime quarter around
the rim of a glass, then dip the rim into the salt.

Add 3–4 ice cubes to the glass and squeeze in the lime juice. Add the tomato
juice, a couple of dashes each of Worcestershire sauce and Tabasco and a little
salt and pepper and stir well.

Top the glass up with Corona, and continue to do so as you drink.

RASPBERRY AND POMEGRANATE 'MARTINIS'

(PICTURED PAGE 248)

These are great for a girly get-together; they look fab and super-pretty.
Use the best vodka you can get — I use an Aussie brand called 666;
the quality is fantastic and the bottle is rather cool, too.

125 g raspberries
60 ml vodka
juice of 1 lime
3 teaspoons sugar syrup (see opposite)
2 tablespoons pomegranate juice
1 handful crushed ice
pomegranate seeds and lemon or lime zest, to garnish

Makes 2

Set aside four or five raspberries for the garnish, then blend
the remainder to a smooth puree in a blender. Push through
a fine-meshed sieve into a bowl and discard the seeds.

Place the puree in a chilled cocktail shaker with the vodka,
lime juice, sugar syrup, pomegranate juice and crushed ice.
Close the shaker and mix well to combine.

To serve, strain the cocktail into a glass and garnish
with the reserved raspberries, pomegranate seeds
and lemon or lime zest.

BASIL JALAPENO MARGARITAS

(PICTURED PAGE 249)

The jalapeno-infused tequila and sugar syrup recipes here make enough for over thirty cocktails, so they're great for parties. You'll need to make the jalapeno-infused tequila 2 days ahead of time to allow the flavours to infuse. If you don't use it all, it will keep for up to 3 months in a sterilised jar, however it does get stronger the longer the chillies are in the tequila, so it's best to remove and discard the chillies after a week or so unless you like rocket-fuel heat!

1 lime, quartered
7–8 large mint leaves, roughly torn
4–5 large basil leaves, roughly torn, plus extra to garnish
3 teaspoons white tequila
1 handful crushed ice
ice cubes, to serve

JALAPENO-INFUSED TEQUILA
500 ml white tequila
2–3 jalapeno chillies, seeded and halved lengthways

SUGAR SYRUP
110 g caster sugar

Makes 2

For the jalapeno-infused tequila, place the white tequila and chillies in a jar with a screw-top lid. Seal tightly and set aside to infuse for 2 days before using.

For the sugar syrup, place the sugar and 125 ml water in a saucepan and bring to a boil, stirring so the sugar dissolves. Reduce the heat to medium and simmer, stirring constantly, for 2 minutes, then set aside to cool completely.

Squeeze the lime quarters into a chilled cocktail shaker, then toss the quarters in as well. Add the herbs and bash everything together with a cocktail muddler or the end of a rolling pin. Add the white tequila, 30 ml of the jalapeno-infused tequila and 20 ml of the sugar syrup, along with a good handful of crushed ice. Close the shaker and mix well to combine.

To serve, strain the cocktail into two glasses half-filled with ice cubes and garnish with extra basil leaves.

A MEXICAN WEEKEND AT MY PLACE

El malo

Blanco

My photography producer Sophie Penhallow is a top girl. She's witty and fun and ridiculously wise beyond her years. Her advice (personal and professional) is always bang-on and she's been amazing to work with over the past three years that her agency, Network, has represented me. So, when I heard Sophie was turning thirty, I decided it was only fitting to throw her a bit of a celebratory birthday bash at my place. Seeing as she's crazy about Mexican food, and there are a few Mexican-inspired dishes in the book (as I've recently gone a bit nuts for all things to do with Mexican food myself), we all got together and had a bit of a fiesta – *arriba*!

With Sydney weather being a little unpredictable at times, especially in autumn, the overall feel of Mexico was somewhat lacking as it rained intermittently the whole day (sad/annoyed face!), but we didn't let that dampen our spirits and partied on from early afternoon until the wee hours.

No Mexican party is complete without a good old piñata-bashing session! Two of my younger blog followers were there, Georgia (fifteen) and Maddie (twelve). They are mad fans of my first book and I was thrilled to meet them. They were a delight to have around and bashed the piñata with incredible gusto – it was hilarious to watch.

Again, I couldn't have done all this without my assistant Alice, and help with the styling from Lou Brassil, who sourced props for the day from a fantastic vintage furniture store in Sydney called Doug Up On Bourke. We also found loads of funky Mexican accessories at Holy Kitsch.

Websites of interest:

douguponbourke.com.au
holykitsch.com.au

EETS

THE MOST ~BLE MEANS OF
~KING PERFEC~ONES, CAKES,
~TRY AND PUD~GS AT HOME.

WEIGHT 6 LB.

~OR BI-CARB SODA SHOULD NOT BE USED~

THICK
·
RICH
·
CREAM

0,5 l.

PRODUCT OF AUSTRALIA REG. NO. 268

HALF GALLON

Devondale
ice cream

VANILLA STRAWBERRY CHOCOLATE

NEAPOLITAN

ARTIFICIALLY COLOURED & FLAVOURED
DEVONDALE CREAM PTY. LIMITED, ST. MARYS, N.S.W.

SPICED APPLE AND SALTED BUTTERSCOTCH PAVLOVA

This one's a bit of a show-stopper! Pavlovas are actually pretty easy to make once you get a bit of practise in. Use an appropriate-sized bowl as a template when drawing the circles on the greaseproof paper.

icing sugar, for dusting
½ lemon
6 free-range egg whites
300 g caster sugar
fine salt
1 teaspoon white vinegar
1 teaspoon cornflour
1 teaspoon cream of tartar
1 teaspoon ground cinnamon
250 g mascarpone
300 ml double cream
1 quantity Salted Butterscotch (see page 283)
80 g flaked almonds, toasted

SPICED APPLE

5 large (800 g) green apples, peeled and cored,
    cut into 2 cm cubes
250 ml prosecco or other sparkling
    white wine
75 g brown sugar
1 star anise
1 teaspoon ground cinnamon
5 cloves
1 vanilla pod, split and seeds scraped

Serves 8

Preheat the oven to 170°C/150°C fan/gas 3 and line three baking trays with greaseproof paper.

Draw an 18–20 cm circle on each sheet of paper with a pencil and dust the inside of each circle with icing sugar to stop the meringue from sticking.

Wipe the inside of the bowl of a stand mixer with the cut-side of the lemon to remove any traces of oil. Add the egg whites and whisk on medium speed for 2–3 minutes or until voluminous and frothy. Increase the speed to high and add the sugar, a tablespoon at a time, beating between additions until the mixture is thick and glossy and holds firm peaks.

Add the salt, vinegar, cornflour, cream of tartar and cinnamon and fold in gently to combine.

Dot a small amount of meringue mixture on the undersides of each corner of the greaseproof paper on the trays to hold it in place. Divide the meringue mixture among the trays, mounding it onto the paper within the circles. Flatten the tops and smooth the sides, then transfer to the oven. Immediately reduce the oven temperature to 140°C/120°C fan/gas 1 and bake for 1¼ hours.

Leave the meringues in the switched-off oven to cool completely with the door slightly ajar.

Meanwhile, for the spiced apple, place all the ingredients in a saucepan along with 125 ml water. Stir to combine, then bring to a boil over high heat. Reduce the heat to low–medium and simmer for 6–7 minutes or until the apple is starting to soften but is still holding its shape.

Remove the apple with a slotted spoon and set aside. Discard the star anise, cloves and vanilla pod, then simmer the remaining liquid over low–medium heat for about 15 minutes or until reduced to a syrupy glaze.

Stir the glaze through the reserved apple and set aside to cool completely.

Whip the mascarpone and cream together until thick and smooth.

To assemble, spread one-third of the cream mixture over the first meringue, top with one-third of the spiced apple, drizzle with one-third of the salted butterscotch and scatter with one-third of the almonds. Gently sandwich a second meringue on top and repeat the layering twice more. Serve immediately.

VANILLA PANNA COTTA WITH RHUBARB AND ROSE COMPOTE

A brilliant dinner-party dessert, this is incredibly easy to prepare and you can make it the night before so it's ready to whip out of the fridge after dinner. Feel free to top with other stewed fruits depending on what is in season.

3 sheets gelatine
350 ml double cream
350 ml milk
75 g caster sugar
1 vanilla pod, split and seeds scraped

RHUBARB AND ROSE COMPOTE
650 g rhubarb, trimmed and cut into 4 cm lengths
125 ml red wine
finely grated zest of 1 orange
2 tablespoons honey
1 tablespoon rosewater
1 sheet gelatine
1 teaspoon caster sugar (optional)

Makes 4

Place the gelatine sheets in a bowl and cover with cold water. Leave to stand for 5 minutes.

Meanwhile, combine the cream, milk, sugar and vanilla seeds in a saucepan. Bring to just below a simmer over low–medium heat, then cook for 5 minutes, stirring often and taking care not to let the mixture boil.

Squeeze out the excess water from the gelatine, then add to the pan and stir over low heat until dissolved. Remove from the heat and set aside to cool for 10 minutes, then pour into four serving glasses and refrigerate for 3–4 hours.

Meanwhile, for the compote, preheat the oven to 200°C/ 180°C fan/gas 6.

Place the rhubarb in a roasting tin just large enough to hold it in a single layer. Add the red wine, orange zest, honey and rosewater and cover with foil. Pop in the oven and cook for 15–20 minutes or until the rhubarb is just tender.

Drain the rhubarb through a sieve placed over a small saucepan to catch the cooking liquid. Set the rhubarb aside to cool completely.

Place the gelatine sheet in a bowl and cover with cold water. Leave to stand for 5 minutes.

Place the saucepan containing the poaching liquid over medium–high heat and bring to a boil. Reduce the heat to medium and simmer for 1–2 minutes or until reduced to approximately 80 ml of liquid.

Squeeze out the excess water from the gelatine, add to the pan and stir over low heat until dissolved. Taste the syrup; if it is very tart, stir in the caster sugar. Remove from the heat and set aside to cool for 15 minutes.

Spoon 1 tablespoon of the syrup over each of the set panna cottas, then divide the rhubarb among the glasses. Refrigerate for 1 hour or until the syrup has set, then serve.

PINK GRAPEFRUIT, TARRAGON AND CINNAMON FRIANDS

I love making friands as they are so quick and easy, and great for morning tea. Tarragon works really well with grapefruit, and the latter adds a nice zing to these little almondy cakes. If you can, try to find a silicone friand pan to make this even easier.

160 g unsalted butter
3 pink or ruby-red grapefruit
100 g plain flour
125 g ground almonds
½ teaspoon ground cinnamon
490 g icing sugar
6 free-range egg whites
5–6 tarragon leaves, very finely chopped

Makes 12

Preheat the oven to 200°C/180°C fan/gas 6 and grease twelve holes of a friand or cupcake tin.

Melt the butter in a small saucepan, then set aside to cool.

Meanwhile, finely grate the zest from one grapefruit, then peel and segment this and one more grapefruit, and set the zest and segments aside. Juice the remaining grapefruit and set aside.

Sift the flour, ground almonds, cinnamon and 250 g of the icing sugar into a large bowl, and make a well in the centre.

In another bowl, whisk the egg whites with a fork for 30 seconds or until frothy. Add to the dry ingredients, along with the cooled melted butter, and combine thoroughly with a wooden spoon. Add the tarragon and reserved zest and combine, then transfer the batter to a jug.

Pour the batter into the prepared friand holes, filling each just over halfway. Bake for 20–25 minutes or until lightly browned. Remove from the oven and leave to cool in the tins for 10 minutes before turning out onto a wire rack to cool completely. Spread out a sheet or two of foil under the rack to catch any icing that may drip down.

Sift the remaining icing sugar into a bowl, add 2½ tablespoons grapefruit juice and blend until smooth. Spoon the icing over the cooled friands and leave to set for 1–2 minutes before topping each one with a grapefruit segment.

CHOCOLATE AND HAZELNUT GELATO

(PICTURED PAGE 272)

The following two gelato recipes were given to me by my gorgeous assistant
and all-round lifesaver, Alice. She has written a book or two on ice creams
and gelatos, and these soft-serve style ones are particularly good. You'll need
a sugar thermometer and an ice-cream maker for both these recipes.

140 g hazelnuts
125 ml double cream
500 ml milk
30 g cocoa powder, sifted
65 g good-quality milk chocolate, coarsely chopped
65 g good-quality dark chocolate, coarsely chopped
150 g caster sugar
1 free-range egg white
1 tablespoon Frangelico (optional)

Serves 4

Preheat the oven to 200°C/180°C fan/gas 6.

Spread the hazelnuts evenly on a baking tray and roast for 10 minutes or until
golden and aromatic. Wrap the hot nuts in a clean tea towel and rub to remove the
skins, then coarsely chop and place in a saucepan.

Add the cream and milk to the pan, place over low–medium heat and bring to just
below boiling point. Remove from the heat and add the cocoa and chopped chocolate,
then whisk until the chocolate has melted and the mixture is smooth. Transfer to
a bowl and set aside to cool, leaving the chopped hazelnuts in the mixture to steep.

Combine the sugar and 60 ml water in a small, heavy-based saucepan and bring to a
boil, stirring regularly. Cook for 2–3 minutes or until the sugar has dissolved and the
temperature registers 120°C on a sugar thermometer.

Meanwhile, whisk the egg white in a stand mixer on high speed for 2 minutes.
With the motor running, slowly pour in the hot sugar syrup; it will be voluminous
and fluffy once incorporated. Continue whisking for 5–8 minutes or until the
mixture is at room temperature.

Strain the hazelnut and chocolate mixture through a fine-meshed sieve into a bowl,
and discard the hazelnuts. Stir in the Frangelico, if using, and add to the egg white
mixture. Whisk briefly until just incorporated. Transfer to a plastic container with
a lid and refrigerate for 2–3 hours (or overnight) to chill completely.

Remove from the freezer and briefly whisk to combine in case the mixture has
separated, then churn in an ice-cream maker until frozen. Freeze for 1–2 hours
before serving. It will keep in the freezer for 3–4 days.

BUTTERMILK GELATO

(PICTURED PAGE 273)

60 ml double cream
250 ml milk
1 vanilla pod, split
170 g caster sugar
1 free-range egg white
500 ml buttermilk

Serves 4–6

Place the cream, milk and vanilla pod in a small saucepan over low–medium heat and bring to just below boiling point. Remove from the heat and set aside to cool.

Combine the sugar and 60 ml water in a small, heavy-based saucepan and bring to a boil, stirring regularly. Cook for 2–3 minutes or until the sugar has dissolved and the temperature registers 120°C on a sugar thermometer.

Meanwhile, whisk the egg white in a stand mixer on high speed for 2 minutes. With the motor running, slowly pour in the hot sugar syrup; it will be voluminous and fluffy once incorporated. Continue whisking for 5–8 minutes or until the mixture is at room temperature, then add the buttermilk and mix just until incorporated.

Discard the vanilla pod from the milk mixture and add to the egg-white mixture. Whisk for about 20 seconds or until combined.

Transfer to a plastic container with a lid and refrigerate for 2–3 hours (or overnight) to chill completely.

Remove from the freezer and briefly whisk to combine in case the mixture has separated, then churn in an ice-cream maker until frozen.

This is best served immediately although it will keep in the freezer for up to 4 days. It is delicious served with fresh berries or a fruit sorbet.

APPLE AND BLACKBERRY HAZELNUT CRUMBLE SQUARES

Another great picnic or school lunch box idea, these squares will keep in an airtight container in the fridge for up to 3 days.

150 g chilled unsalted butter, chopped
300 g plain flour, sifted
165 g caster sugar
1 free-range egg, lightly whisked
1 teaspoon vanilla extract
2 green apples, peeled, cored and chopped
250 g fresh or frozen blackberries (thawed if frozen)
juice of 1 lime

HAZELNUT CRUMBLE
75 g plain flour
100 g chilled unsalted butter, chopped
75 g brown sugar, plus 2 tablespoons extra, for sprinkling
45 g rolled oats
125 g toasted skinned hazelnuts (see page 164), chopped
½ teaspoon ground ginger

Serves 12

Whiz the butter, flour and 110 g of the caster sugar in a food processor until the mixture resembles fine breadcrumbs. Add the egg and vanilla and whiz again to combine. Shape the dough into a ball, then wrap in cling film and refrigerate for 20 minutes.

Meanwhile, place the apple, blackberries, lime juice, remaining caster sugar and 125 ml water in a large saucepan. Bring to a boil, then reduce the heat to medium and simmer for 15–20 minutes or until the apple is soft and most of the liquid has evaporated. Remove from the heat and leave to cool, then puree with a hand-held blender until smooth. Set aside.

Preheat the oven to 200°C/180°C/gas 6 and grease and line a 24 cm ×x 30 cm baking tin with greaseproof paper.

For the crumble, whiz the flour and butter in a food processor until the mixture resembles breadcrumbs. Add the remaining ingredients and pulse to combine, then set aside.

Remove the dough from the fridge, unwrap and flatten into a disc. Place between two pieces of greaseproof paper and roll out to a 24 cm ×x 30 cm rectangle, then use to line the tin.

Prick the base all over with a fork, then bake for 20 minutes or until starting to brown. Leave to cool for 5 minutes, then spread the pureed fruit mixture over the base. Scatter over the crumble, then sprinkle with the extra brown sugar. Bake for 25–30 minutes or until the crumble top is golden. Allow to cool in the tin for 30 minutes or until firm, then cut into squares and serve.

GLUTEN-FREE LEMON AND COCONUT CAKE

This cake was a massive hit on the blog when I featured it a while back, so I just had to include it, plus I adore the shot; it's one of my faves. If you like, you can cut the cake in half horizontally and sandwich together using half the icing, then top with the remaining icing, or just ice the whole cake as I've done here. You can buy gluten-free flour and coconut flour from health food stores and some supermarkets.

2½ tablespoons coconut flour
125 g gluten-free plain flour
1 teaspoon baking powder
150 g unsalted butter, softened
150 g caster sugar
3 free-range eggs
1 tablespoon milk
60 ml lemon juice
80 g sour cream
100 g shaved coconut flakes

LEMON CREAM-CHEESE ICING
250 g cream cheese, softened
320 g icing sugar, sifted
finely grated zest of 1 lemon
3 teaspoons lemon juice

Serves 8

Preheat the oven to 180°C/160°C fan/gas 4 and grease and line an 18 cm springform tin.

Sift the flours and baking powder into a bowl and set aside.

Cream the butter and sugar in a stand mixer for 8–10 minutes until light and fluffy. Add the eggs, one at a time, beating between each addition. Add the milk, lemon juice, sour cream and sifted dry ingredients and beat on low–medium speed until smooth and combined.

Spoon into the prepared tin and smooth the top. Place on the middle shelf of the oven and bake for 15 minutes, then increase the oven temperature to 200°C/180°C fan/gas 6 and bake for a further 30–35 minutes or until a skewer comes out clean when inserted in the middle.

Remove from the oven and leave to cool in the tin for 15 minutes before turning out onto a wire rack to cool completely.

For the icing, beat the cream cheese in a stand mixer for 2–3 minutes. Add the icing sugar, lemon zest and juice and beat for 5–6 minutes until light, thick and creamy. Transfer to a bowl, cover and chill in the fridge for 1 hour to thicken.

Spread the icing over the top and sides of the cooled cake, then cover with shaved coconut and serve immediately.

SELF-SAUCING MOCHA PUDDING

If you're a chocaholic who loves gooey, fudgy choctastic puddings, then this one's for you! Serve it warm with fresh cream or a good vanilla ice cream.

100 g plain flour
2 teaspoons baking powder
25 g cocoa powder
75 g brown sugar
1¼ tablespoons strong espresso coffee
100 ml milk
1 free-range egg
50 g unsalted butter, melted
1¼ tablespoons creme de cacao (optional)
whipping cream or vanilla ice cream, to serve

MOCHA SAUCE
75 g brown sugar
1 tablespoon cocoa powder, sifted
1 teaspoon espresso instant coffee powder
250 ml boiling water

Serves 4

Preheat the oven to 200°C/180°C fan/gas 6 and butter a 1 litre capacity pudding bowl.

Sift the flour, baking powder and cocoa into a large bowl, then add the sugar and stir to combine. Add the coffee, milk, egg, melted butter and creme de cacao, if using, and stir to combine thoroughly with a wooden spoon. Pour into the prepared pudding bowl and place on a baking tray.

To make the sauce, place the sugar, cocoa and coffee powder in a bowl and stir to combine. Scatter evenly over the pudding, then pour the boiling water over the top.

Bake for 25–30 minutes or until the pudding has risen and the sauce bubbles up around the sides. Serve warm with cream or vanilla ice cream.

THE QUEEN'S PUDDING BOILER
CHALLIS'
No 16
PATENT

VICTORIA SPONGE WITH LIMONCELLO AND BALSAMIC STRAWBERRIES

This is my take on the classic '4, 4, 4 and 2' Victoria sponge recipe that my mum used to make. Strawberries pair very well with lemon, and this recipe uses the Italian lemon liqueur, limoncello, which you'll find at Italian delis and selected liquor stores.

175 g unsalted butter, softened
175 g caster sugar
3 free-range eggs
1 teaspoon vanilla extract
175 g self-raising flour, sifted
1 tablespoon milk
1 tablespoon limoncello or 2 teaspoons lemon juice
200 g mascarpone
100 ml whipping cream
icing sugar, for dusting

LIMONCELLO AND BALSAMIC STRAWBERRIES
400 g strawberries, hulled and quartered
2 tablespoons caster sugar
2 tablespoons limoncello or 1 tablespoon lemon juice
2 teaspoons balsamic vinegar
1 small handful mint, finely chopped

Serves 8

Preheat the oven to 200°C/180°C fan/gas 6 and grease and line two× 20 cm springform tins.

Cream the butter and sugar in a stand mixer for 5–6 minutes or until pale and creamy. Add the eggs, one at a time, beating between additions.

Add the vanilla and half the flour and beat until incorporated. Add the milk and limoncello or lemon juice and beat to combine, then add the remaining flour and beat until combined.

Divide the batter between the prepared tins and smooth the tops, then gently tap the tins on the benchtop to remove any air bubbles. Bake for 20–25 minutes or until the tops are golden brown and a skewer comes out clean when inserted into the centre of each cake.

Remove from the oven and leave the cakes to cool in the tins for 5 minutes, before turning out onto wire racks to cool completely.

Meanwhile, for the limoncello strawberries, place the strawberries, sugar, limoncello or lemon juice and balsamic vinegar in a small saucepan. Bring to a boil over high heat, then reduce the heat to low, add the mint and simmer for 2–3 minutes (the fruit should be soft but still holding its shape).

Drain the mixture, reserving the syrup. Set the strawberries aside in a bowl. Return the syrup to the pan and place over medium heat. Simmer until reduced by half, then pour over the strawberries and leave to cool completely.

Whisk together the mascarpone and cream until smooth and thick enough to hold its shape. Spread the mascarpone cream over one cake and place on a serving platter large enough to catch any juices from the filling. Top with the strawberry mixture, then sandwich the second sponge on top and dust liberally with icing sugar.

YOU'LL ENJOY
M. Polaner's

DOUBLE CHOC BROWNIES WITH SALTED BUTTERSCOTCH AND CHERRIES

These are incredibly naughty. You can cut them into squares, or into larger pieces and serve them warm for a dinner-party dessert with a good vanilla ice cream. When you are adding the butterscotch layer, don't worry if it blends into the batter a bit, just spread it out as best you can. The side bits are the best as the caramel goes all sticky and chewy!

110 g unsalted butter, melted and cooled a little
1 tablespoon kirsch liqueur or 1 teaspoon vanilla extract
110 g caster sugar
3 free-range eggs
110 g plain flour
½ teaspoon baking powder
50 g cocoa powder, sifted
2 tablespoons milk
100 g good-quality dark chocolate, finely chopped
250 g sour or morello cherries from a jar, drained well
icing sugar, for dusting

SALTED BUTTERSCOTCH
150 g brown sugar
250 ml double cream
75 g unsalted butter, cubed
¼ teaspoon sea salt, crushed

Serves 12

Preheat the oven to 200°C/180°C fan/gas 6 and grease and line the base and sides of a 28 cm ×x 18 cm ×x 3 cm baking tin.

For the salted butterscotch, place all the ingredients in a saucepan and bring to a boil, stirring often. Reduce the heat to low—medium and simmer for 15—20 minutes until thickened and smooth, then set aside to cool slightly.

Place the melted butter, kirsch or vanilla, sugar and eggs in a bowl and mix together. Sift in the flour, baking powder and cocoa and combine well with a wooden spoon. Mix in the milk, then fold in the chocolate and cherries.

Spoon half the batter into the prepared tin and smooth the top. Dollop with salted butterscotch, then top with the remaining batter. Bake for 35—40 minutes or until cooked through and the top is cracked a little.

Remove from the oven and leave to cool completely in the tin before cutting into squares. Dust with icing sugar before serving.

THE MOST FLAVORFUL

PINE NUT, LEMON AND POPPY-SEED COOKIES

№. 284

These lovely little buttery cookies are quick and easy to make. Sometimes I serve them without the filling; they're perfect with a cup of tea or to pair with a lemon mousse at a dinner party. The cookies themselves will keep for up to 7 days stored in an airtight container; sandwiched cookies will keep in an airtight container in the fridge for up to 4 days.

225 g self-raising flour
¼ teaspoon ground ginger
3 free-range egg whites
165 g caster sugar
110 g butter, melted and cooled
finely grated zest of ½ lemon
75 g pine nuts, plus extra to scatter on top
1 tablespoon poppy seeds

LEMON AND CREAM-CHEESE FILLING
125 g cream cheese, softened
75 g unsalted butter, softened
160 g icing sugar, sifted
finely grated zest of ½ lemon
2 teaspoons lemon juice

Makes 35

Preheat the oven to 180°C/160°C fan/gas 4 and line two large baking trays with greaseproof paper.

Sift the flour and ground ginger into a bowl, stir to combine and set aside.

Beat the egg whites in a stand mixer on high speed until frothy. With the motor running, gradually add the sugar, about a tablespoon at a time, and whisk to firm peaks. Fold in the butter, lemon zest, pine nuts and poppy seeds with a large metal spoon. Gently fold in the flour mixture in two or three batches until incorporated.

Spoon the mixture into a large piping bag fitted with a 1.5 cm plain round nozzle. Pipe 3 cm dots onto the prepared trays at 6 cm intervals, then gently press the tops to smooth the surface. Scatter with the remaining pine nuts and poppy seeds, pressing them down slightly to help them stick.

Bake for 10–12 minutes or until golden brown around the edges, then remove and leave to cool slightly before transferring to wire racks to cool completely.

Meanwhile, for the filling, beat the cream cheese and butter in a bowl until smooth, then add the icing sugar, lemon zest and juice and combine until light and fluffy. Spoon into a piping bag fitted with a 1 cm round or star-shaped nozzle and chill in the fridge for 15 minutes.

To assemble, pipe some filling onto the flat side of half the cookies, then sandwich together with a second cookie, gently twisting the top one as you push down. Refrigerate for 1 hour before serving.

DOUBLE CHOC CHEESECAKE WITH BERRY SAUCE

I like to use Arnott's Chocolate Ripple biscuits for the biscuit base here, but you could also use Oreo cookies; just bung them in whole, there's no need to scrape off the cream in the centres first. If you don't want to use amaretto, you can substitute 1 teaspoon of vanilla extract. Leave some of the cherry stems attached for a nicer presentation, if you like.

250 g plain (un-iced) chocolate biscuits
125 g blanched almonds
120 g unsalted butter, melted and cooled
100 g good-quality dark chocolate
100 g good-quality milk chocolate
500 g cream cheese, softened
250 g light sour cream
4 free-range eggs
250 g dark brown sugar
300 ml double cream, plus extra, whipped, to serve
1 tablespoon amaretto

BERRY SAUCE

250 g fresh cherries (pitted, if you like) or sour cherries from a jar, drained well
1 × 250 g punnet strawberries, hulled and halved
1 × 125 g punnet raspberries
1 tablespoon lime juice
2 tablespoons caster sugar

Serves 8

Preheat the oven to 170°C/150°C fan/gas 3 and grease and line the base and sides of a 22 cm springform cake tin. Wrap the outside of the tin with foil, sealing it securely.

In a food processor, whiz the biscuits and almonds to fine crumbs. Add the butter and pulse to combine. Press this mixture evenly into the base of the prepared tin and chill in the fridge for 30 minutes.

Melt the dark and milk chocolate in a heatproof bowl that fits snugly over a saucepan of gently simmering water, then set aside to cool slightly.

Beat the cream cheese and sour cream in a stand mixer on low–medium speed for 1–2 minutes until smooth and combined. Add the eggs, one at a time, beating after each addition until incorporated. Add the brown sugar, cream and amaretto and beat on low speed for 1 minute. Beat in the melted chocolate until combined.

Pour the batter onto the biscuit base and tap the tin gently on a flat surface to remove any bubbles. Place the cake tin in a large roasting tin and pour enough cold water into the roasting tin to come 2–3 cm up the sides of the cake tin. Carefully transfer to the oven and bake for 1½ hours or until set at the edges with a slight wobble in the centre. Leave in the switched-off oven to cool for 1 hour with the door slightly ajar, then remove and cool to room temperature, before chilling in the fridge for 1 hour.

Meanwhile, for the berry sauce, place all the ingredients in a saucepan, bring to a boil, then reduce the heat to low–medium and simmer for 3 minutes or until the fruit is soft but still holding its shape. Drain for 5 minutes over a bowl, reserving the syrup. Place the syrup in the pan and simmer over medium heat for 10 minutes or until thick and glossy, then gently fold into the fruit and set aside to cool completely.

Sit the cheesecake on a large plate and remove the tin, then top with berry sauce and serve with whipped cream.

BERRY ALMOND COBBLER

I used fresh fruit for this, but you can use frozen raspberries and blueberries if you wish; the result will be just as good. I've had this classic American dessert a few times on my travels in the US; this is my own take on all the delicious cobblers I've enjoyed over the years.

2 × 250 g punnets strawberries, hulled, halved if large
3 × 125 g punnets blueberries
2 × 125 g punnets raspberries
55 g caster sugar
1 teaspoon cornflour
fine salt
finely grated zest and juice of 1 lime
2 tablespoons brown sugar
70 g slivered almonds, toasted
double cream, to serve

COBBLER TOPPING
300 g plain flour
1 teaspoon baking powder
1 teaspoon cream of tartar
3 tablespoons brown sugar
½ teaspoon ground cinnamon
pinch of fine salt
120 g unsalted butter, chilled and cubed
180 ml buttermilk
1 tablespoon double cream
1 tablespoon amaretto (optional)

Serves 6

Preheat the oven to 200°C/180°C fan/gas 6.

For the topping, whiz all the dry ingredients in a food processor. Add the butter and mix until it resembles coarse breadcrumbs.

Whisk together the buttermilk, cream and amaretto in a bowl, then add to the butter mixture and whiz until the mixture just comes together. Set aside.

Combine all the berries in a bowl and stir in the sugar, cornflour, a pinch of salt, the lime zest and juice. Transfer to a baking dish (I use a 28 cm round dish that is about 6 cm deep) and spread out evenly. Top with large clumps of the cobbler dough (don't spread this out evenly; this is part of the charm). Sprinkle over the brown sugar and slivered almonds, then bake for 40–45 minutes or until the top is golden brown.

Serve hot with double cream.

UPSIDE-DOWN PLUM CHIFFON CAKE

If plums aren't in season, you can use tinned plums instead; just drain them well and pat them dry with kitchen roll. This cake may sink a little when you remove it from the oven but don't worry, you'll be flipping it over anyway.

8 plums, pitted, quartered lengthways
1 stick cinnamon
290 g caster sugar
4 free-range eggs, separated, plus 2 egg whites, extra
60 ml olive oil
100 ml milk
1 teaspoon vanilla extract
150 g plain flour
60 g ground almonds
1 teaspoon baking powder
pinch of cream of tartar
whipped cream, to serve

Preheat the oven to 180°C/160°C fan/gas 4 and grease and line the base and sides of a 22 cm springform tin. Place the tin on a foil-lined baking tray.

Arrange the plum quarters, cut-side down, in an even layer over the base of the prepared tin.

Place the cinnamon stick, 150 g of the sugar and 225 ml water in a heavy-based saucepan and bring to a boil over high heat. Cook for 8–10 minutes (swirl the pan often but do not stir) until the caramel starts to turn golden brown, then carefully pour the hot caramel over the plums in the tin. Remove the cinnamon stick with tongs and discard.

Combine the egg yolks, oil, milk and vanilla in a large mixing bowl with a wooden spoon. Sift the flour, ground almonds, baking powder and 70 g of the sugar into a separate bowl and combine. Add this to the egg-yolk mixture and beat with a wooden spoon to form a thick batter.

Beat the six egg whites in a metal bowl with hand-held electric beaters until thick and frothy. Add the remaining sugar in three or four batches, beating well after each addition. When the mixture is thick, frothy and voluminous, add the cream of tartar and fold in with a large metal spoon.

Spoon one-third of the egg-white mixture into the cake batter and fold in gently, then add the remaining egg-white mixture and fold in gently to combine.

Pour the batter over the plums, then transfer to the oven and bake for 50–60 minutes or until a skewer inserted in the centre comes out clean.

Leave to cool in the tin for 15 minutes before slicing and serving warm with whipped cream.

Serves 8–10

SHEEP'S MILK CHEESECAKE WITH MANGO AND PEANUT

Sheep's milk yoghurt is available from gourmet delis and selected supermarkets, but you can use natural yoghurt if you can't find it. Make sure you start this the day before you want to eat it, as the cheesecake needs to be refrigerated in the tin overnight so it is firm enough to slice.

120 g raw unsalted peanuts
250 g digestive biscuits
100 g unsalted butter, melted and cooled
500 g cream cheese, softened
4 free-range eggs
220 g caster sugar
400 g sheep's milk yoghurt
125 ml double cream
1 tablespoon plain flour
2 ripe mangoes, peeled, flesh cut away from the stone
1 tablespoon lime juice

Serves 8–10

Preheat the oven to 200°C/180°C fan/gas 6 and grease and line a 24 cm springform cake tin. Wrap the outside of the tin with foil, sealing it securely.

Scatter the peanuts on a baking tray lined with greaseproof paper. Roast for 10–12 minutes or until golden brown, then remove and leave to cool for 5 minutes before transferring to the bowl of a food processor. Add the biscuits and whiz together for 1–2 minutes or until broken down into fine crumbs. Add the melted butter and whiz again until well combined. Press this mixture evenly into the base of the prepared tin and chill in the fridge for 30 minutes.

Reduce the oven temperature to 170°C/150°C fan/gas 3.

Beat the cream cheese in a stand mixer on high speed until smooth and creamy. Add the eggs, one at a time, beating after each addition until incorporated. Add the sugar, yoghurt, cream and flour and beat on medium–high speed for 1–2 minutes to combine thoroughly.

Puree the mango flesh in a blender, then add the lime juice and stir to combine.

Pour the batter onto the biscuit base and tap the tin gently on a flat surface to remove any air bubbles. Pour the mango puree into the filling in a spiral motion and, using a fork, gently swirl the puree into the filling. Place the cake tin in a large roasting tin and pour enough cold water into the roasting tin to come 2–3 cm up the sides of the cake tin.

Carefully transfer to the oven and bake for 1½ hours or until set at the edges with a slight wobble in the centre. Leave in the switched-off oven to cool completely with the door slightly ajar.

Cover and chill overnight before serving.

BELGIAN SHORTBREAD

I enjoyed this dessert at a Christmas dinner a few years ago,
and although I normally don't like dates, I loved them in this!
You get the crumbly pastry, sweet and sticky dates and crunchy
flaked almonds; I couldn't get enough of it . . .

125 g unsalted butter, chilled
75 g caster sugar
225 g self-raising flour
¼ teaspoon sea salt
1 free-range egg, separated
1–2 teaspoons milk (optional)
100 g raspberry or plum jam
100 g plump moist dates, pitted and chopped
40 g slivered almonds

Serves 8

Preheat the oven to 170°C/150°C fan/gas 3 and grease and line a 25 cm
round tart tin with a removable base.

Place the butter, sugar, flour and salt in a food processor and blend
until the mixture resembles fine breadcrumbs. Add the egg yolk and
pulse until the mixture just comes together (add a little milk if the
mixture is too dry). Turn out onto a floured surface and knead into
a ball. Wrap in cling film and chill in the fridge for 30 minutes.

Divide the chilled dough in half. Roll out one portion between two
sheets of greaseproof paper into a round the right size to fit inside the
tin; don't worry if it's not a perfect circle, as it will all come together
as it cooks. Gently drape the pastry over the rolling pin and transfer to
the tin, pressing it down.

Place the jam in a bowl and press down with the back of a spoon until
smooth and softened.

Spread the jam evenly over the pastry in the tin and cover with the
chopped dates. Roll out the second portion of dough in the same way
as the first and lay on top of the dates. Beat the egg white and brush
over the pastry, then sprinkle with the slivered almonds, pushing
them down slightly.

Bake for 40–45 minutes, then cool completely in the tin or on a wire
rack before cutting into wedges to serve.

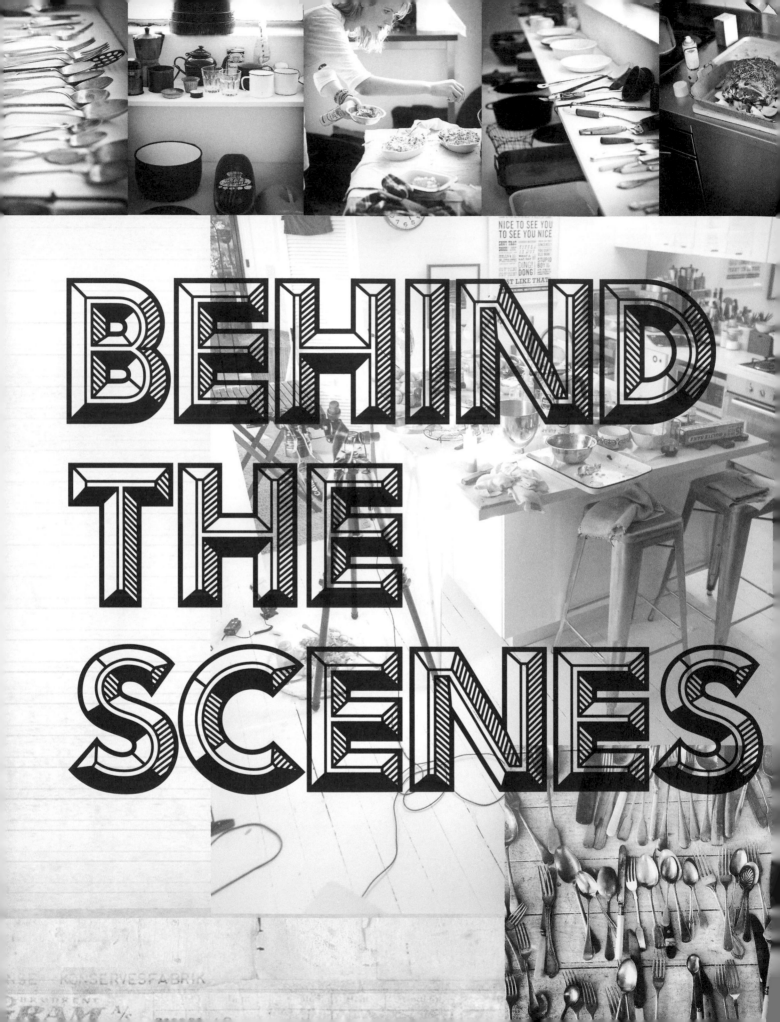

BEHIND THE SCENES

Alice

Katie

ANDY

You will need ...

1 kg uncooked prawns, peeled an[d]
tails intact
Juice of 2 limes
Sea salt and freshly ground black pepper
2 limes, halved
Extra lime quarters and crusty bread, to serve

For the Thai dipping sauce ...

2 cloves garlic, crushed
2 tablespoons fish sauce
3 tablespoons lime juice
2 tablespoons brown sugar
½ small red onion, finely diced
1 long red chilli, finely chopped
1 long green chilli, finely chopped
1 tablespoon chopped coriander
1 tablespoon chopped mint
1 x 1 cm piece ginger, finely grated
Pinch sea salt and freshly ground black pepper

SOUP €5
ED CARROT
FENNEL
VEG €6.50
ANDWICH
COURGETTE,
A, ROAST TOMATO
EEN PESTO
MEAT €7
ANDWICH
IZO, ROAST RED
, TZATZIKI
PECIALS
FFED AUBERGINE
FETA 8
LENTILS 8
SALAD €9.50

I want to say an enormous thank you to all the people who have helped me complete this book over the past year.

Most importantly, to my amazing assistant, Alice Cannan. If it wasn't for you, I don't think there would even be a second book! You are an incredible assistant and friend. Thank you for all those trips to the supermarket, all the washing up, chopping veg, cooking, handing me things on set before I even knew I needed them, and for helping to make what is often an immensely stressful situation a much calmer one.

To everyone at Penguin Australia – Julie, Virginia, Katrina, Evi O, Daniel and Elena – again, without your input, we may not be reading these pages.

To Nick Banbury, quite possibly THE world's best recipe tester! Nick, thank you for your diligence and perfectionism: I have accumulated a wealth of knowledge from you. I am chuffed to have been paired with someone who possesses such an amazing knowledge of all things food.

To all my friends back home in Ireland, in NYC, elsewhere around the globe and here in Australia, you know who you are – you've been so supportive throughout the book process and, most importantly, through a very tough time personally in early 2014.

To my 'Rozelle gang': Michelle, Andy and Colin – your unending friendship and support means the world to me. I would be lost without you three.

To all my incredible friends in the Barossa: Jan and John Angas; Michael Wohlstadt; Caroline and Donna; David and Jennifer; Fiona and Mel – thank you for all your help, support and hospitality. I look forward to the next glass/bottle of red at Hutton Vale!

To Madeleine Mouton: thanks again, M, for being there just when I needed you.
To Lou Brassil for your amazing styling help. To all the super 'Weekend Girls' Lunch' blog readers – your enthusiasm and great spirit on the day was invaluable and I so enjoyed meeting you all.

To Sophie, my photo producer, for being a great friend, a good laugh and juggling jobs for me with the busy book schedule.

To Georgie and all the girls at Major & Tom: once again, Georgie, your support and friendship is greatly cherished.

To Vlad, the coolest courier in Sydney. Prop collection and return would have been hellish without your chilled-out, 'nothing is ever a problem' nature.

To Chris the butcher at Darling Street Meats: thanks for supplying the best meat in town and for prepping it all so perfectly for me.

To everyone mentioned above, this book is totally dedicated to you all.

To my sister Julie, Claudio, Erika, Colm, Leonie and Tim – I love you all endlessly.

Thank you from the bottom of my heart. xx

First published in Great Britain in 2015 by Saltyard Books
An imprint of Hodder & Stoughton
An Hachette UK company

1

First published by Penguin Group (Australia), 2014

A CIP catalogue record for this title is available from the British Library.

ISBN 978 1 473 61188 7
Ebook ISBN 978 1 473 61189 4

Book design by Katie Quinn Davies
Design, photography, propping and styling: Katie Quinn Davies
Main assistant: Alice Cannan
General assistants: Marita Cranwell, Amber De Florio, Louise Masters, Madeleine Mouton,
Michaela Wolf and Jahde Zinzopoulos
Second photographer for A Mexican Weekend At My Place: Dan Gosse
Styling assistant for A Weekend Girls' Lunch and A Mexican Weekend At My Place: Lou Brassil
Colour separation by Splitting Image Colour Studio, Clayton, Victoria
Typeset in Filosofia by Post Pre-press Group, Brisbane, Queensland

Printed and bound in China by 1010 Printing International Ltd

Hodder & Stoughton policy is to use papers that are natural, renewable and recyclable products and made from wood grown in sustainable forests. The logging and manufacturing processes are expected to conform to the environmental regulations of the country of origin.

Saltyard Books
338 Euston Road
London NW1 3BH

www.saltyardbooks.co.uk